SMALL ME

José Saramago was born in Portugal in 1922 and became a full-time writer in 1979. His oeuvre included plays, poetry, short stories, non-fiction and over a dozen novels, which have been translated into forty languages and established him as Portugal's greatest contemporary writer. In 1998 he was awarded the Nobel Prize for Literature. José Saramago died on 18 June 2010.

Margaret Jull Costa has translated works by many leading Spanish and Portuguese writers, and her translations have brought her several prizes, among them the Oxford Weidenfeld Translation Prize for José Saramago's *All the Names* and the Premio Valle-Inclán for Bernado Atxaga's *The Accordionist's Son.*

ALSO BY JOSÉ SARAMAGO IN ENGLISH TRANSLATION

Fiction

The Manual of Painting and Calligraphy
Baltasar & Blimunda
The Year of the Death of Ricardo Reis
The Gospel According to Jesus Christ
The History of the Siege of Lisbon
Blindness
All the Names
The Tale of the Unknown Island
The Stone Raft
The Cave
The Double
Seeing
Death at Intervals

Non-fiction
Journey to Portugal

JOSÉ SARAMAGO

Small Memories

TRANSLATED FROM THE PORTUGUESE BY
Margaret Jull Costa

VINTAGE BOOKS
London

Published by Vintage 2010

2 4 6 8 10 9 7 5 3 1

Copyright © José Saramago and Editorial Caminho, SA, Lisbon 2006
by arrangement with Literarische Agentur Dr. Ray-Güde Mertin, Inh.
Nicole Witt e.K., Frankfurt am Main, Germany

English translation copyright © Margaret Jull Costa 2009

José Saramago has asserted his right under the Copyright, Designs
and Patents Act 1988 to be identified as the author of this work

This book is sold subject to the condition that it shall not,
by way of trade or otherwise, be lent, resold, hired out,
or otherwise circulated without the publisher's prior
consent in any form of binding or cover other than that
in which it is published and without a similar condition,
including this condition, being imposed on the
subsequent purchaser

First published with the title *As Pequenas Memórias* in 2006 by
Editorial Caminho, SA, Lisbon

First published in Great Britain in 2009 by
Harvill Secker

Vintage
Random House, 20 Vauxhall Bridge Road,
London SW1V 2SA

www.vintage-books.co.uk

Addresses for companies within The Random House Group Limited
can be found at: www.randomhouse.co.uk/offices.htm

The Random House Group Limited Reg. No. 954009

A CIP catalogue record for this book
is available from the British Library

ISBN 9780099520481

This publication was assisted by a grant from the Direcção-Geral do
Livro e das Bibliotecas / Portugal

The Random House Group Limited supports The Forest
Stewardship Council (FSC), the leading international forest
certification organisation. All our titles that are printed on
Greenpeace approved FSC certified paper carry the FSC logo.
Our paper procurement policy can be found at:
www.rbooks.co.uk/environment

Mixed Sources

Product group from well-managed
forests and other controlled sources
www.fsc.org Cert no. TT-COC-2139
© 1996 Forest Stewardship Council

Printed and bound in Great Britain by
CPI Bookmarque, Croydon, CR0 4TD

For Pilar, who had not yet been born

and who took so long to arrive

Let yourself be led by the child you were.

From *The Book of Exhortations*

The village is called Azinhaga and has, so to speak, been where it is since the dawn of nationhood (it had a charter as early as the thirteenth century), but nothing remains of that glorious ancient history except the river that passes right by it (and has done, I imagine, since the world was created) and which, as far as I know, has never changed direction, although it has overflowed its banks on innumerable occasions. Less than half a mile from the last houses, to the south, the Almonda, for that is the name of my village's river, meets the Tejo, which (or, if you'll allow me, whom) it used to help, in times past and as far as its limited volume would allow, to flood the fields when the clouds unleashed the torrential winter rains, and the dams upstream, brimful and bursting, were obliged to discharge the excess of accumulated water. The land around there is flat, as smooth as the palm of your hand, with no orographic irregularities to speak of, and any dykes that were built served not so much to contain the powerful rush of the river when it floods as to guide it along a course where it would cause least damage. From those distant days onwards, the people born and bred in my village learned how to deal with the two rivers that shaped its character, the Almonda, which slips past its feet, and the more distant Tejo, half-hidden behind the wall of poplars, ash trees and willows that accompany it, and, for good reasons and bad, both rivers are omnipresent in the memories and conversations of every family. It was here that I came into the world and it was from here, when I was not yet two years old, that my parents, migrants driven by necessity, carried me off to Lisbon and to other ways of feeling, thinking and living, as if my having been born in the village were merely the result of some mistake made by chance, some momentary lapse on the part of destiny, a lapse for which destiny still had the power to make amends. This proved not to be the case. The child, unnoticed, had already put out tendrils and sent down roots, and there had been time for that fragile child-seed to place his tiny, unsteady feet on the muddy ground and to receive from it the indelible mark of the earth, that shifting backdrop to the vast ocean of air, of that clay, now dry, now wet, composed of vegetable and animal remains, of detritus left behind by everything and everyone, crushed and pulverised rocks, multiple, kaleidoscopic substances that passed through life and to life returned, just like the suns and the moons, times of flood and drought, cold weather and hot, wind and no wind, sorrows and joys, the living and the not. Only I knew, without knowing I did, that on the illegible pages of destiny and in the blind meanderings of chance it had been written that I would one day return to Azinhaga to finish being born. Throughout my childhood and my early adolescence, that poor, rustic village, with its murmuring frontier of green trees and water, with its low houses surrounded by the silver-grey of olive trees, sometimes scorched by the burning summer sun, sometimes gripped by the murderous winter frosts or drowned by the floodwaters that came in through the front door, was the cradle in which my gestation was completed, the pouch into which the small marsupial withdrew to make what he alone could make, for good or possibly ill, of his silent, secret, solitary self.

The experts say that the village was born and grew up along a path, an *azinhaga*, which comes from the Arabic word '*as-zinaik*' meaning 'narrow street', but, taken literally, that couldn't have been true in those early days, because a street, be it wide or narrow, is still a street, whereas a path can never be more than a short-cut, a way of reaching your destination more quickly, a route which, generally speaking, has no future and no great ambition to be any longer than it is. I don't know at what point the widespread cultivation of olive trees was introduced into the region, but I'm sure, because the older villagers told me so, that some of the most ancient of those trees would have seen two or possibly three centuries pass them by. They will see no more though. A few years ago, acres and acres of land planted with olive trees were ruthlessly cleared, hundreds of thousands of trees were cut down, ripped from the deep soil, or else the old roots of trees that had given light to lamps and flavour to stews were left to rot. The landowners, most of them owners of vast estates, were paid by the European Union per tree uprooted, and now, in place of the mysterious and vaguely troubling olive groves of my childhood and adolescence, in place of the gnarled trunks covered in moss and lichen and full of holes in which the lizards could hide, in place of the canopies of branches laden with black olives and with birds, what we see is one enormous, monotonous, unending field of hybrid maize, all grown to the same height, possibly with the same number of leaves per stem, and tomorrow perhaps with the exact same arrangement and number of ears and the same number of kernels on each ear. I'm not complaining, I'm not bemoaning the loss of something that didn't even belong to me, I'm simply trying to explain that this present-day landscape isn't mine, it isn't the place where I was born, I didn't grow up there. As we all know, maize is a vital crop, more important for many people than olive oil, and I myself, when I was a boy, in the years of my early adolescence, would walk the maizefields after the workers had finished harvesting, with a cloth bag slung around my neck, picking the ears they had missed. I must confess, however, that I now take a somewhat wicked pleasure – a revenge I neither sought nor wanted, but which came to meet me of its own accord – when I hear the people in the village say that it was a mistake, a huge blunder, to have got rid of the old olive groves. No point now, I think, crying over spilt oil. And they tell me that new olive trees are now being planted, but of a sort which, however long they live, will never reach any great height. This variety grows more quickly, and its lack of height makes it easier to pick the olives. What I don't know is where the lizards will go.

The child I was did not see the landscape as the adult he became would be tempted to see it from the lofty height of manhood. The child, while he was a child, was simply *in* the landscape, formed part of it and never questioned it, never said or thought, in these or other words: 'What a beautiful landscape, what a magnificent panorama, what a fabulous view!' Naturally, when he climbed the stairs to the church belfry or scrambled to the top of a sixty-foot ash tree, his young eyes were capable of appreciating and noticing the wide open spaces before him, but it must be said that he was always more drawn to singling out and focussing on things and beings that were close, on what he could touch with his hands, on what offered itself to him as something which, without him being aware of it, demanded to be understood and absorbed into his spirit (the latter being a jewel which, needless to say, the child had no idea he carried within him): a snake slithering away, an ant carrying on high a crumb of wheat, a pig eating from the trough, a toad lolloping along on bent legs, or a stone, a spider's web, the soil turned up by the blade of the plough, an abandoned bird's nest, the drop of resin running like a tear down the trunk of a peach tree, the frost glittering on the undergrowth. Or the river. Many years later, using the words of the adult he then was, the adolescent would write a poem about that river – a humble stream of water that is now polluted and fetid – where he had bathed and which he had navigated. He called it 'Protopoem' and here it is: 'Out of the tangled skein of memory, out of the darkness of its inextricable

7

knots, I tug at what appears to be a loose end./Slowly I pull it free, afraid it might fall to pieces in my fingers./It's a long thread, green and blue, and smells of slime, warm and soft as living mud./It's a river./It drenches my now wet hands./The water flows over my outspread palms, and suddenly I'm not sure if the water is flowing out of me or washing over me./I continue to tug at the thread, which is not just a memory now, but the actual body of the river itself./Boats sail over my skin, and I am the boats and the sky above them, and the tall poplars that slide serenely across the luminous film of my eyes./Fish swim in my blood and hesitate between staying too near the surface and plumbing the depths, just like the vague summonses issued by memory./I feel the strength of my arms and the pole that prolongs them./It pushes down into the river and into me like a slow, steady heartbeat./ Now the sky is nearer and has changed colour./It's all green and full of singing because the songs of birds are springing awake on every branch./And when the boat stops in a large clearing, my naked body gleams in the sun, among the still brighter light igniting the surface of the waters./There, memory's confused recollections and the suddenly revealed face of the future fuse into one truth./ A nameless bird appears out of nowhere and perches silently on the stiff prow of the boat./I wait motionless for the whole river to be bathed in blue and for the birds on the branches to explain to me why the poplars are so tall and their leaves so full of murmurings./Then, with the body of the boat and the river safely back in the human dimension, I continue on toward the golden pool surrounded by the raised swords of the bullrushes./ There I will bury my pole two feet down in the living rock./A great primordial silence will fall when hands join with hands./And then I will know everything.' No one can know everything or ever will, but there are moments when we're capable of believing that we will, perhaps because at that moment, soul, consciousness, mind, or whatever you care to call the thing that makes us more or less human, was filled to overflowing. I gaze down from the bank at the barely moving current, the almost stagnant water and, absurdly, I imagine that everything would go back to being as it was if only I could once again plunge my childhood nakedness into the river, if I could grasp in today's hands the long, damp pole or the sonorous oars of yesteryear, and propel across the water's smooth skin the rustic boat that used to carry, to the very frontiers of dreams, the being I was then and whom I left stranded somewhere in time.

The house where I was born no longer exists, not that it matters, because I have no memory of having lived in it. The other house, the impoverished dwelling of my maternal grandparents, Josefa and Jerónimo, has also disappeared beneath a mound of rubble, the house which, for ten or twelve years, was my true home, in the most intimate and profound sense of the word, the magical cocoon in which the metamorphoses vital to both the child and the adolescent took place. That loss, however, has long since ceased to cause me any suffering because, thanks to the memory's reconstructive powers, I can, at any moment, rebuild its white walls, replant the olive tree that shaded the entrance, open and close the low front door and the gate to the vegetable garden where I once saw a small snake coiled and waiting, or I can go into the pigsties and watch the piglets suckling, enter the kitchen and pour from the jug into the chipped mug the water which, for the thousandth time, will quench that summer's thirst. Then I say to my grandmother: 'Grandma, I'm going for a walk.' And she says: 'Off you go, then', but she doesn't warn me to be careful, no, in those days, grown-ups had more confidence in the children they brought up. I put a slice of cornbread and a handful of olives and dried figs in my bag, grab a stick just in case I have to fend off some canine attack, and set off into the countryside. I don't have many routes to choose from: it's either the river and the almost inextricable vegetation that clothes and protects its banks or the olive groves and the hard stubble of the recently harvested wheat, or the dense thicket of tamarisks, beeches, ash trees and poplars that flank the Tejo downstream, beyond the point where it meets the Almonda, or else, to the north, about three or four miles from the village, the Paul do Boquilobo, a lake, pond or pool that the creator of these landscapes neglected to carry off to paradise. There wasn't much choice, it's true, but for the melancholy child, for the contemplative and often sad adolescent, these were the four quarters into which the universe was divided – indeed, each was a universe in itself. The adventure could last hours, but never finished until I had achieved my goal. To cross alone the burning expanses of the olive groves, to cut a difficult path through the bushes, treetrunks, brambles and climbers that raised thick walls along the banks of the two rivers, to sit and listen in a shady clearing to the silence of the woods broken only by the piping of the birds and the creaking of the branches in the wind, to travel across the pond by scrambling from branch to branch of the weeping willows that grew in the water; these, you will say, are not feats deserving of special mention in an age like ours, in which, by the age of five or six, any child, however sedentary and indolent, who is born in the civilised world, has already travelled to Mars to crush however many little green men he may encounter, has decimated the terrible army of mechanical dragons guarding the gold in Fort Knox, has blown tyrannosaurus rex to smithereens, has plumbed the deepest of submarine trenches without benefit of diving-suit or bathyscaphe, and has saved humankind from the monstrous meteorite that was heading straight for Earth. Beside such superior exploits, the little boy from Azinhaga could only offer his ascent to the topmost branch of the sixty-foot ash tree or, more modestly, but affording far greater pleasure to the palate, climbing the fig tree in the yard, early in the morning, to pick the fruit while it was still wet with dew and to sip, like a greedy bird, the drop of honey that oozed from within. Small beer perhaps, but then that heroic conqueror of tyrannosauruses would doubtless be incapable of catching a lizard in his bare hands.

Many people solemnly state, supporting their words with some authoritative quotation from the classics, that landscape is a state of mind, which, put into ordinary words, must mean that the impression made on us by contemplating any landscape is always dependent on our temperamental ups and downs and on whatever mood, cheerful or irascible, we happen to be in at the precise moment when that landscape lies before us. Now far be it from me to disagree, but this assumes that states of mind are the exclusive property of the mature adult, of grown-ups, of those people who are already capable of using, more or less correctly, the kind of grave concepts necessary to analyse, define and tease out such subtleties, the property of adults, who think they know everything. For example, no one ever asked that adolescent what kind of mood he was in or what intriguing tremors were being recorded on the seismograph of his soul when, one unforgettable morning, while it was still dark, he emerged from the stable, where he had slept among the horses, and his forehead, face and body, and something beyond the body, were touched by the white light of the most brilliant moon that human eyes had ever seen. Nor what he felt when, with the sun already up, while he was herding the pigs across hill and vale on his way back from the market where he had managed to sell most of them, he realised that he was walking across a stretch of rough paving made from apparently ill-fitting slabs of stone, a strange discovery in the middle of an area that seemed to have lain deserted and empty since the beginning of time. Only much later, many years afterwards, would he realise that he had been walking along what must have been the remains of a Roman road.

Nevertheless, these marvels, both mine and those of the precocious manipulators of virtual universes, are as nothing compared with the time when, just as the sun was setting, I left Azinhaga and my grandparents' house (I would have been about fifteen then) to go to a distant village, on the other side of the Tejo, in order to meet a girl with whom I thought I was in love. An old boatman called Gabriel (the villagers called him Graviel) took me across the river; he was red from the sun and from the brandy he drank, a kind of white-haired giant, as sturdily built as St Christopher. I had sat down to wait for him on this side of the river, on the bare boards of the jetty, which we called the port, while I listened to the rhythmic sound of the oars on the surface of the water as it was touched by the last light of day. He was approaching slowly, and I realised (or was it just my state of mind?) that this was a moment I would never forget. A little way along from the jetty on the other side was an enormous plane tree, beneath which the estate's herd of oxen used to sleep out the siesta hours. I set off to the right, cutting across fallow fields, low walls, ditches, through puddles and past maizefields, like a stealthy hunter on the trail of some rare beast. Night had fallen, and the only sound in the silence of the countryside was that of my footsteps. As to whether the encounter with the girl proved a happy one or not, I will tell you later. There was dancing and fireworks, and I think I left the village close on midnight. A full moon, although less splendid than that earlier one, lit everything around. Before I reached the point where I would have to leave the road and set off across country, the narrow path I was following seemed suddenly to end and disappear behind a large hedge, and there before me, as if blocking my way, stood a single, tall tree, very dark at first against the transparently clear night sky. Out of nowhere, a breeze got up. It set the tender stems of the grasses shivering, made the green blades of the reeds shudder and sent a ripple across the brown waters of a puddle. Like a wave, it lifted up the spreading branches of the tree and, murmuring, climbed the trunk, and then, suddenly, the leaves turned their undersides to the moon and the whole beech tree (because it was a beech) was covered in white as far as the topmost branch. It was only a moment, no more than that, but the memory of it will last as long as my life lasts. There were no tyrannosauruses, Martians or mechanical dragons, but a meteor did cross the sky (which is not so hard to believe), although, as became clear afterwards, mankind was never at risk. After walking for a long time, and with dawn still far off, I found myself in the middle of the countryside, standing outside a roughly built shack. There, to stave off hunger, I ate a piece of mouldy cornbread someone else had left behind, and there I slept. When I woke in the first light of morning and emerged, rubbing my eyes, to find a luminous mist obscuring the fields all around, I felt – if I remember rightly, and always assuming I'm not just making it up – that I had finally been born. High time.

Where does my fear of dogs come from? And my fascination with horses?

The fear – which even today, and despite recent happy experiences, I can barely control when face to face with an unfamiliar representative of the canine species – comes, I am sure, from the utter panic I felt as a seven-year-old, when, one night as darkness was falling and the street-lamps were already lit and just as I was about to go into the house on Rua Fernão Lopes, in the Saldanha district of Lisbon, where we lived along with two other families, the street door burst open and through it, like the very fiercest of Malayan or African beasts, came the neigh-bours' Alsatian dog, which immediately began to pursue me, filling the air with its furious, thunderous barking, while I, poor thing, desperately dodged behind trees to avoid him as best I could, meanwhile calling for help. The aforementioned neighbours – and I use the word only because they lived in the same building as us, not because they were the equals of nobodies like us who lived in the attic room on the sixth floor – took longer to restrain their dog than even the most elementary charity demanded. Meanwhile – if my memory is not deceiving me, and I'm not being misled by my humiliation and my fear – the owners of the dog, young, refined, elegant (they must have been the teenage children of the family, a boy and a girl) were, as people used to say then, laughing fit to burst. Fortunately, I was quick on my feet, and the animal never caught me, still less bit me, or perhaps that wasn't its intention; it had probably been startled to find me standing outside the door. We were both afraid of each other, that's what it was. The intriguing thing about this otherwise banal episode is that I knew, when I was standing outside the front door, that the dog, that particular dog, was waiting there to go for my throat. Don't ask me how, but I knew.

And the horses? My problem with horses is a more painful one, of the kind that leaves a permanent wound in a person's soul. One of my mother's sisters, Maria Elvira by name, was married to a certain Francisco Dinis, who worked as a keeper on the Mouchão de Baixo estate, part of Mouchão dos Coelhos, the name given to the whole of a particularly large estate on the left bank of the Tejo, more or less in a direct line with a village called Vale de Cavalos or Vale of Horses. Anyway, to return to my Uncle Francisco. Working as a keeper on such a large and powerful estate meant that he belonged to the aristocracy of the countryside: double-barrelled shotgun, green beret, white shirt buttoned up to the neck regardless of whether it was blazing hot or freezing cold, red belt, knee-high leather boots, short jacket and, naturally, a horse. Now, in all those years – and from eight until fifteen is a lot of years – it never once occurred to my uncle to lift me up into that saddle and I, presumably out of a kind of childish pride of which I couldn't even have been aware, never asked him to do so, however much I wanted him to. I can't remember by what circuitous route (possibly because she knew another of my mother's sisters, Maria da Luz, or one of my father's sisters, Natália, who had worked as a maid for the Formigal family in Lisbon's Estrela district, in Rua dos Ferreiros, a street in which, an eternity later, I, too, would live), but one day, a lady, still fairly young, moved into Casalinho, as my maternal grandparents' house had always been known; she was, as people used to say then, the 'lady friend' of a gentleman who owned a shop in Lisbon. She was unwell and in need of rest, which is why she had come to spend a little time in Azinhaga, to breathe in the good country air and, in so doing, improve by her presence and her money the food that we ate. With this same woman, whose name I can't quite remember (perhaps it was Isaura, or perhaps Irene, no, it was Isaura), I enjoyed several enjoyable bouts of hand-to-hand combat and a few arm-wrestling matches, which always ended with me (I must have been about fourteen at the time) throwing her down onto one of the beds in the house, chest to chest, pubis to pubis, while my grandmother Josefa, whether knowingly or innocently I'm not sure, would laugh out loud and say how strong I was. The woman would sit up, excited and flushed, smoothing her dishevelled hair and swearing that if we had been fighting for real, she wouldn't have allowed herself to be beaten. Fool or utter innocent that I was, I could have taken her at her word, but never dared. Her relationship with the shopkeeper was a well-established one, proof of which was their pale, wan seven-year-old daughter, who had come with her mother to enjoy the fresh air. Now, my uncle was a small, very upright man, a bit of a bully at home, but docility personified when it came to dealing with bosses, superiors or city-dwellers. It was no surprise, then, that he should bow and scrape to our visitor, behaviour that might have been taken as evidence of the natural politeness of country folk if it hadn't smacked more of servility than simple respect. One day, my uncle, may he rest in peace, obviously wanted to show how fond he was of our two female visitors and so he picked up the little girl, placed her in the saddle and, playing groom to her little princess, paraded her up and down in front of my grandparents' house, while I watched in silent anger and humiliation. Some time after this, on an end-of-term trip with the technical school from which, a year later, I would emerge as a qualified general mechanic, I rode one of the sad old horses you can hire in Sameiro, hoping that by doing so I might perhaps make up in adolescence for the treasure denied me in childhood: the joy of an adventure that had come so close I could have touched it, but that had remained forever out of reach. Too late. The scrawny nag took me wherever it fancied, stopped whenever it cared to and didn't even turn its head to say goodbye when I slid down from the saddle, feeling just as sad as I had on that other occasion. The house where I live now is full of images of horses. Guests visiting for the first time almost always ask if I'm a keen rider, when the truth is that I'm still suffering from the effects of a fall from a horse I never rode. There are no outward signs, but my soul has been limping for the last seventy years.

One cherry brings another cherry, and just as a horse brought an uncle, an uncle will bring with him a rural version of the final scene of Verdi's *Otello*. As was the case with most of the older houses in Azinhaga (and I am, of course, speaking of those inhabited by the lesser folk), my aunt and uncle's house in Mouchão dos Coelhos – built, it should be said, on a stone base at least six feet high, with an external staircase, to keep the house safe from the winter floods – consisted of two rooms, one usually facing onto the road (or in this case onto fields), which we called the *casa-de-fora* or outside room, the other being the kitchen, with a door leading out into the yard at the back, again via a staircase, made of wood this time and plainer than the front stairs. My cousin José Dinis and I used to sleep in the kitchen, in the same bed. He was three or four years younger than me, but even though the difference in age and strength was entirely in my favour, this didn't stop him getting into fights with me whenever it seemed to him that I, his older cousin, was trying to outdo him in gaining the favour, whether explicit or implicit, of the local girls. I will never forget the torment of jealousy the poor boy went through over a girl from Alpiarça called Alice, a pretty, delicate creature who went on to marry a young tailor and, many years later, came to live in Azinhaga with her husband, who continued to work in the trade. When I was in the village on holiday once and learned that she was living there, I passed by her door unseen and, for the briefest of moments, barely long enough to glance in, all those past years rose up before me. She was sitting with her head bent over her sewing and didn't see me, and so I never found out whether or not she would have recognised me. I should also say that even though José Dinis and I fought like cat and dog, I had often known him to hurl himself to the floor and weep desperate tears when the holidays were over and I was saying goodbye to the family in order to return to Lisbon. He wouldn't even look at me, and if I tried to approach, he would repel me with kicks and punches. My Aunt Maria Elvira was quite right when she said of her son: 'He's a bad boy, but he has a good heart.'

José Dinis had solved the problem of squaring the circle without once seeking advice on tackling that most difficult of operations. He was a bad boy, but he had a good heart.

Jealousy was evidently a disease that ran in the Dinis family. During harvest-time, but also when the melons were beginning to ripen and the kernels of maize were hardening on the cobs, Uncle Francisco rarely spent a whole night at home. On horseback, his shotgun across his saddle, he would patrol the vast estate, on the look-out for felons, major or minor. I imagine that if he did feel the need for a woman, whether under the lyrical influence of the moon or due to the friction of saddle on crotch, he would trot home, quickly relieve that particular itch, rest a little from the effort, then return to his night patrol. One unforgettable day, in the early hours, my cousin and I were fast asleep, exhausted from the day's various fights and forays, when Uncle Francisco irrupted like a fury into the kitchen, brandishing his shotgun and yelling: 'Who's been in here?' At first, barely conscious after being so violently wrenched from sleep, I could just make out through the open door the double bed and my aunt sitting up in her white nightdress, clutching her head and moaning: 'The man's mad! The man's mad!' He was not perhaps mad, but he was certainly in the grip of jealousy, which comes pretty much to the same thing. He was saying that he would kill us all if we didn't tell him the truth about what had happened, and he kept urging his son to answer, come on, come on, but José Dinis' courage, amply proven in everyday life, failed him completely when confronted by his father armed with a shotgun and almost foaming at the mouth. I told my uncle that no one had come into the house, that we had, as usual, gone to bed immediately after supper. 'But what about later, can you swear to me that no one else was here?' bawled the Othello of Mouchão de Baixo. I began to grasp what was going on, my poor Aunt Maria Elvira was begging me: 'Tell him, Zezito, tell him, because he won't believe me.' I think that was the first time in my life that I gave my word of honour. It was comical really, a boy of fourteen giving his word that his aunt had not taken another man into her bed, as if I, who slept like a log, would have noticed (no, I mustn't be so cynical, Aunt Maria Elvira was a thoroughly decent woman), but the fact is that the very solemnity of that word of honour had the desired effect, I suppose because it was so novel, and also because when country people spoke, oaths and curses apart, they meant what they said and didn't waste their breath on flowery rhetoric. My uncle finally calmed down, leaned his shotgun against the wall, and it became clear what had happened. They slept in one of those brass bedsteads with brass rails at the head and the foot, the ends of which were held in place by spherical brass knobs that screwed into the side bars. Clearly, those internal screws had become worn with use and lost their grip. When my uncle came in and turned up the wick on the oil-lamp, he had seen what he thought was proof of his dishonour: the rail at the head of the bed had worked loose and hung like an accusing finger over the sleeping woman's head. Aunt Maria Elvira must have raised her arm as she turned over in bed and dislodged the brass rail. I could not at the time imagine what shameful, shocking orgies Francisco Dinis must have imagined, what writhing bodies convulsed by every conceivable erotic extravagance, but the fact that the poor man lacked the intelligence to know which way the wind was blowing, or if indeed there was any wind, shows to what extent jealousy can blind someone to the obvious. Had I been of the cowardly race of Iagos (I know nothing, I saw nothing, I was asleep), then perhaps the night silence in Mouchão de Baixo would have been shattered by two gunshots, and an innocent woman would have lain dead between sheets that had never known any other masculine smells or fluids than those of the wife-murderer himself.

I remember that this same uncle would turn up now and then carrying a rabbit or a hare, shot during his patrols of the estate. As a keeper, there was no closed season as far as he was concerned. One day, he returned home as triumphant as a crusader who has just vanquished an army of infidels. He had a large bird slung over the saddle tree, a grey heron, a creature new to me and which I believe was a protected species. Its meat was rather dark and tasted faintly of fish, unless, after all these years, I am imagining tastes that never tickled my palate or passed my gullet.

Another edifying story from Mouchão de Baixo involved Pezuda, a woman whose real name I've long forgotten, if, indeed, I ever knew it, and who was called Pezuda – Big Foot – because she had truly enormous feet, a misfortune she could not conceal because, like all of us (young children and women, that is), she went everywhere barefoot. Pezuda lived right next door to my uncle and aunt, and she and her husband had a house exactly like theirs (I can't remember now if they had any children), and as so often happened in that place – where for good or ill, I was, in the most exact sense of the expression, brought up body and soul – the two families were at daggers drawn, they didn't get on, they didn't speak, not even to say good morning. (My grandmother Josefa's neighbour, in the Divisões, or Divisions, district of the village – so-called because the olive trees that grew there were owned by someone else – was one of my grandfather Jerónimo's sisters, Beatriz by name, and yet, even though they were of the same blood, they had entirely broken off relations and had hated each other for more years than my childhood memory could comprehend. I never found out the reason for the quarrel that had separated them.) Pezuda's real name, of course, appeared in the baptismal records in the church and in the register of births, marriages and deaths, but to us she was simply Pezuda, and that ugly nickname said it all. So much so that on one famous occasion (when I was about twelve), I was sitting at the door of the house, at the top of the steps, when she, the hated neighbour, passed by (I only hated her out of a mistaken sense of familial solidarity, because the woman had never done me any wrong), and I commented to my aunt, who was inside sewing:

'There's old Pezuda going by.' I said this more loudly than I'd intended, and Pezuda heard me. From down below, full of righteous indignation, she proceeded to give me a piece of her mind, saying I was a badly brought-up Lisbon brat (and I was anything but a Lisbon brat), who, it would seem, had not been taught to respect his elders, a moral quality essential to the smooth functioning of society. She rounded off her rebuke by saying that she would tell her husband about me when he returned from work at sunset. And I must confess that I spent the rest of the day with heart pounding and stomach churning, fearing the worst, because her husband had a reputation as a real bruiser. I decided privately that I would make myself scarce until after dark, but Aunt Maria Elvira was on to me at once, and just as I was about to disappear, she said very calmly: 'When it's time for him to come home from work, you sit at the door and you wait. If he tries to beat you up, I'll be here, but don't move from that spot.' That is the nature of all really useful lessons, the sort that last a lifetime, that place a hand on your shoulder just when you're about to give in. I remember that it was a gorgeous sunset (and it really was, this isn't a mere literary afterthought), and I sat there at the door, watching the red clouds and the violet sky, with no idea what might happen, but convinced that the day would end badly for me. Eventually, when the sun had set, Pezuda's husband arrived home, went up the stairs to his house, and I thought: 'This is it.' But he didn't come out again. I still don't know what went on inside. Was it that when his wife told him what had happened, he decided that it wasn't worth taking seriously anything a mere lad had said? Had she been generous enough not to say a word to her husband about the unfortunate episode and decided to swallow the insult hurled at a pair of feet that were hardly her fault anyway? Had she thought of all the scornful names she could call me, 'stammerer', for example, but had chosen instead, out of charity, to keep silent? The truth is that when my aunt summoned me to supper, I wasn't filled only with a sense of satisfaction. Oh, I was glad that I'd managed to pretend a courage that was, in fact, merely borrowed, but I also had the uncomfortable feeling that I'd missed out on something.

Would I really have preferred to have had my ears boxed or been given a good spanking, which I was still of an age to receive? Well, no, my thirst for martyrdom didn't go that far. I'm sure, though, that something that night was left hanging in the air. Or, rather, as I write about it now, perhaps I'm wrong. Perhaps the attitude of those hated neighbours in Mouchão dos Coelhos was simply the second lesson I needed to learn.

It's time to explain the reasons behind the original title I gave to this memoir – *The Book of Temptations* – which, at first sight, and indeed at second and third sight, seems to have nothing to do with the matters dealt with so far nor, it must be said, with those I will touch on later. My initial ambitious idea – from the days when I was working on *Baltasar and Blimunda* all those years ago – had been to show how sainthood, that 'monstrous' manifestation of the human spirit, disturbs, confuses and disorients nature, and is capable of subverting our permanent and apparently indestructible animality. It seemed to me at the time that the crazed saint depicted by Hieronymus

Bosch in his *Temptation of St Anthony* had, by the mere fact of being a saint, drawn up from the depths all the forces of nature, visible and invisible, the mind's most grotesque and most sublime thoughts, lusts and nightmares, every hidden desire and every manifest sin. Oddly enough, my attempt to transpose such a thorny subject (I soon realised that my literary gifts fell far short of such a grandiose project) onto a simple repository of reminiscences that clearly called for a more modest title, didn't mean that I hadn't at some point found myself in a similar situation to that of the saint. For as a creature of the world, I must also be the seat of all desires and the object of all temptations, simply because 'it goes with the territory'. What difference would it make if we were to replace St Anthony with a child, an adolescent or an adult? Just as the saint was besieged by imaginary monsters, I, as a child, was subject to the most appalling night terrors, and the naked women who continue to cavort lasciviously around all the Anthonys of the world are no different from the fat prostitute who, one night, as I was on my way to the Cinema Salão Lisboa, alone as usual, asked me in a weary, indifferent voice: 'Do you want to come up to my room?' That was in Rua do Bem-Formoso, next to the flight of steps there, and I must have been about twelve. And while it's true that some of Bosch's phantasmagoria make any comparison between saint and child seem ludicrous, this is perhaps only because we don't remember or don't wish to remember what went on in our heads as children. That flying fish which, in Bosch's painting, carries the saint through air and wind, is not so very different from our body flying in dreams, as mine often did through the gardens separating the buildings in Rua Carrilho Videira, grazing the tops of the lemon trees and medlar trees or rising up with a simple flap of the arms and hovering above the rooftops. And I can't believe that St Anthony experienced worse terrors than, for example, the recurring nightmare in which I found myself locked in a triangular room with no furniture, doors or windows, but where there was 'something' (I call it that because I never did find out what it was) gradually growing in size while a piece of music played, always the same music, and the thing grew and grew until I was trapped in one corner, at which point I would wake, terrified, in the grim silence of the night, struggling for breath and drenched in sweat. Nothing of great note, you might say. Maybe that's why this book changed its name and became *Small Memories*. Yes, the small memories of when I was small.

Let's move on. The Barata family entered my life when we moved from 57 Rua dos Cavaleiros to Rua Fernão Lopes. In February 1927, we were, I think, still living in the Mouraria district of Lisbon, because I have a vivid memory of hearing artillery fire whistling over the roof from the Castelo de São Jorge and intended for the rebels encamped in Parque Eduardo VII. A straight line drawn from the castle esplanade, and taking as an intermediate point the building in which we were living, would bring you infallibly to the traditional command post of all Lisbon's military insurrections. Hitting your target or not would simply be a question of taking careful aim and adjusting your sight. Given that my first school was in Rua Martens Ferrão and primary education began at the age of seven, we must have left the house in Rua dos Cavaleiros shortly after I began my studies. (There is another and possibly more likely hypothesis to consider, one that I set down here before continuing: that those shots came not from the uprising of 7 February 1927, but from another, the following year. Indeed, although I may have started going to the cinema early on in my life – to the aforementioned Salão Lisboa, better known as the 'Fleapit' and located in the Mouraria, next to the Arco do Marquês de Alegrete – I certainly wouldn't have done so at the tender age of barely five, my age in February 1927.) Of the people with whom we shared a house in Rua dos Cavaleiros my only clear memory is of the couple's son. His name was Félix and I experienced one of my worst night-time horrors with him, doubtless brought on by the hair-raising films we used to watch then, and which would now seem laughable.

The Baratas were two brothers, one of whom was a policeman, like my father, although the former belonged to a different branch called Criminal Investigation.

My father, who would reach the rank of sergeant a few years later, was, at the time, a simple constable in the PSP, the Public Security Police, working either on foot patrol or at the police station, depending on which shift he was on and, unlike the Barata brother, who was always in plain clothes, he bore his identification number on his collar, 567. I can remember that as clearly as if I were seeing it now, the brass numbers on the stiff collar of his dolman, as the jacket of his uniform was known, made of grey ticking in the summer and thick blue woollen cloth in the winter. The name of the Barata brother who was in the Criminal Investigation Department was António, and he wore a moustache and was married to a woman called Conceição, who, years later, brought him certain problems, for my mother suspected, or may even have had proof, that my father and Conceição had enjoyed a degree of intimacy unacceptable even to the most tolerant of minds. I never discovered what really happened, I speak only of what I could deduce and imagine from the few hints dropped by my mother, when we were already living in the new house. Indeed, that might have been the real reason behind our move from Rua Padre Sena Freitas, where we were all living, to Rua Carlos Ribeiro, both of which were in the area being built on the hill that goes down from the Igreja da Penha de França to the beginning of Vale Escuro. And I only left Rua Carlos Ribeiro when I was twenty-two, to marry Ilda Reis.

I remember rather less about the other Barata brother, but I can still see him, small, round and rather plump. If I ever knew what he did for a living, I have long since forgotten. I think his wife's name was Emília and his, I believe, was José: having been buried for years beneath many layers of forgetting, those names, like that of the supposedly flighty Conceição, rose obediently from the depths of memory when summoned by necessity, like a cork float held fast on the river bed, but which suddenly breaks free of the accumulated mud. They had two children, Domitília and Leandro, both slightly older than me and both with stories to tell, and in the case of Domitília, to my great good fortune, with some sweet memories to recall. Let's begin with Leandro. At the time, he didn't seem particularly intelligent, in fact, he didn't seem very intelligent at all or else made no effort to appear so. His Uncle António Barata, who never wasted his breath on circumlocutions, metaphors or evasions, called him a fool straight out. In those days, we all had to learn from the *Cartilha Maternal* – the *Mother's Primer* – written by João de Deus, who, in his lifetime, enjoyed a deserved reputation as both an excellent person and a wonderful teacher, but who had, whether intentionally or not, given in to the sadistic temptation to strew his lessons with various lexical traps, or perhaps, out of sheer ingenuousness, it simply never occurred to him that they could be perceived as traps by those catechumens less well fitted by nature to deal with the mysteries of reading. We were living, at the time, in Rua Carrilho Videira, on the corner of Rua Morais Soares, and I remember the tempestuous lessons Leandro received from his uncle and which always ended in Leandro receiving several hard slaps (as with the palmer or ferrule, also known as the 'girl with five eyes', the slap was considered an indispensable educational tool) each time poor Leandro encountered a particularly abstruse word, which, as I recall, he never once managed to pronounce correctly. The fateful word was '*acelga*' – meaning Swiss chard – which he pronounced '*a cega*'. His uncle would roar: '*Acelga*, you fool, *acelga*!' and Leandro, already braced and ready to be cuffed round the ear, would repeat: '*A cega*'. Neither his uncle's aggression nor Leandro's dreadful anxiety achieved anything, for even if they had threatened him with death, he would still have said '*a cega*'. Leandro was, of course, dyslexic, but that word, while it might have appeared in the dictionaries of the day, was unknown to the primer written by our good and much-loved João de Deus.

As for Domitília, we were caught one day together in bed, playing at what brides and bridegrooms play at, active and curious about everything on the human body that exists in order to be touched, penetrated and fiddled with. When I try to pinpoint what age I was then, I think I must have been about eleven or perhaps slightly younger (I can't be certain because we lived twice in Rua Carrilho Videira, in the same house). We two bold creatures (who knows which of us had the idea, although it's likely that the initiative came from me) were spanked on the bottom, purely as a formality I think and not very hard. I'm sure the three women in the house, including my mother, would have laughed about it afterwards, behind the backs of the precocious sinners who had been unable to wait until the proper time for such intimate discoveries. I remember crouching on the balcony at the back of the house (on a very high fifth storey), crying, with my face pressed between the railings, while Domitília, at the other end, accompanied me in my tears. But we didn't learn our lesson. A few years later, by which time I was living at 11 Rua Padre Sena Freitas, she went to visit Aunt Conceição, and it happened that not only were my aunt and uncle not in, my parents were out as well, and so we had plenty of time for more detailed investigations, which, although they didn't go all the way, left us both with unforgettable memories, at least in my case, for even now I can see her, naked from the waist down.

Later on, when the two Barata brothers were already living in Praça do Chile, I would go and visit them, my sights set on Domitília, but since, by then, we were both grown up and fully equipped, we found it hard to find a moment alone. It was also in Rua Padre Sena Freitas that I slept (or didn't sleep) part of the night with a slightly older girl cousin (she had the same name, Maria da Piedade, as my mother, who as well as being her aunt was also her godmother) when we were put in the same bed, head to toe. A vain precaution on the part of our ingenuous mothers. While they returned to the kitchen and resumed the conversation we weren't supposed to hear and which they had interrupted in order to take us to bed, where they had covered us up and tucked us in with their own fond hands, we, after a few minutes of anxious waiting, hearts pounding, underneath the sheet and the blanket, in the dark, began a meticulous, mutual, tactile exploration of our bodies with more than justifiable urgency and eagerness, but in a way that was not just methodical, but also, in the circumstances, as instructive as we could make it from the anatomical point of view. I remember that the first move on my part, the first attack, so to speak, brought my right foot into contact with Piedade's already bushy pubis. We were pretending to sleep like angels when, later that night, Aunt Maria Mogas, who was married to a brother of my father's called Francisco, came to get her up and take her home. Ah, yes, those were innocent times.

We must have lived in Rua Padre Sena Freitas for two or three years. That was where we were living when the Spanish Civil War broke out. The move to Rua Carlos Ribeiro must have happened in 1938, or perhaps even 1937. And unless my still, for the moment, serviceable memory allows different dates and references to surface, it's hard, not to say impossible, for me to place certain events in time, but I'm sure that the next incident I'm going to tell you about took place before the war in Spain. A very popular game at the time among the lower classes, one that anyone could make at home (I had hardly any toys, and those I had were made of tin and had been bought in the street from itinerant sellers), consisted of a small rectangular board with twenty-two nails hammered into it, eleven on each side, distributed much as footballers used to be before the emergence of modern tactics, that is, five in front, the forwards, three behind them, the midfielders, also known as halves, two others, known as defenders or backs, and finally the goalkeeper. You could play the game using a marble or, better still, a ball bearing, which you guided in between the nails with a small spatula, then pushed it between two posts (because there were goalposts too) and thus scored a goal. People, both children and grown-ups, had enormous fun with these very meagre materials, and hard-fought contests and championships were fought. Seen from this distance, it seems, and perhaps very briefly was, a golden age. Not that this was always the case, as you will see. One day, my father and I were on the rear balcony playing (I recall that families with few possessions spent most of their time at the back of the house, mainly in the kitchen), I was sitting on the ground and he on a small wooden bench of the kind that was commonplace then and considered indispensable, especially to the women of the household, who sat there to do their sewing. Standing behind me, watching the game, was António Barata. My father was not a man to let his son beat him and so, implacably, and taking advantage of my limited skill, he scored goal after goal. Barata, as an officer in the Criminal Investigation Department, must have had plenty of training in different ways of putting psychological pressure on the detainees in his care, but clearly thought it a good idea to use that occasion to get in a little extra practice. He kept nudging me with his foot from behind and saying: 'You're losing, you're losing.' The boy I was at the time put up for as long as he could with the father who kept winning and the neighbour who kept taunting him, but eventually, in desperation, he struck Barata on the foot (well, 'struck' is too strong a word to describe a blow dealt by a mere child) and at the same time vented his frustration by using the few words that could be spoken in such circumstances without offending anyone: 'Stop it!' Barely were the words out of his mouth, however, than his all-conquering father slapped him twice across the face, so hard that the blow sent him rolling across the concrete floor of the balcony. After all, he had shown disrespect for an adult. Neither father nor neighbour, both of whom were policemen and honest guardians of public order, ever understood that *they* had shown a lack of respect for someone who would have a lot of growing up to do before he could finally tell this sad tale. His and theirs.

From that same balcony, some time later, I courted a girl called Deolinda, who was about three or four years older than me, and who lived in a building in a street that ran parallel to ours, Travessa do Calado, and the back of which looked out onto our house. I should make it clear that this was never a courtship proper, in the sense of my asking for her hand and making more or less lasting promises ('Would you like to go out with me?' 'Certainly, if your intentions are honourable.'). We just looked and waved at each other and talked from balcony to balcony over the intervening yards and washing lines, but we never made any serious commitment. I may have been shy and awkward by nature, but on the occasions when I visited her house (I seem to recall she lived with her grandparents), I went there ready for anything or everything. Both anything and everything turned out to be nothing. She was very pretty, with a small round face, but, to my dismay, had very bad teeth, and, besides, she must have thought me far too young for her to entrust her tender feelings to me. She was amusing herself a little for lack of any better suitor, although, unless I have been much mistaken all these years, I think she regretted that the age difference was so marked. In the end, I gave up the enterprise. Besides, her surname was Bacalhau – salt cod – and I, apparently already sensitive to the sounds and meanings of words, didn't want my wife to go through life burdened with a name like Deolinda Bacalhau Saramago.

I have explained elsewhere how and why I acquired the name of Saramago. How Saramago was not a family name from my father's side, but the nickname – meaning wild radish – by which the family was known in the village. How when my father went to the registry office in Golegã to declare the birth of his second son, the clerk (who was called Silvino) was drunk (although my father always claimed Silvino acted out of pure spite) and he, under the influence and without anyone noticing this onomastic deception, decided to add Saramago to the plain José de Sousa that my father intended me to be. And, as it turned out, thanks to what was clearly divine intervention, on the part, that is, of Bacchus, the god of wine and of those who drink too much of it, I later had no need to invent a pseudonym with which to sign my books. I was very lucky indeed not to have been born into one of the families in Azinhaga, which, at the time and for many years afterwards, had to put up with far more scurrilous nicknames – Pichatada, Curroto and Caralhana – all of which referred to various parts of the male anatomy, namely cock, bum and balls. My family was unaware that I had entered life marked by the name of Saramago until I was seven, for it was only when they had to present my birth certificate in order to enrol me in primary school that the raw truth surfaced from the bureaucratic depths, to the great indignation of my father, who, since moving to Lisbon, had grown to dislike the nickname. The worst of it was that, since – as was apparent from his papers – he was called plain José de Sousa, the Law, ever strict and suspicious, wanted to know why it was that his son was called José de Sousa Saramago. Feeling intimidated and wanting to make sure that everything was right and proper, my father had no alternative but to re-register himself under the name of José de Sousa Saramago. This must, I imagine, be the only case in the whole history of humanity of a son giving his name to his father. Not that it helped us or humanity very much, because my father, steadfast in his antipathies, always insisted on being called plain Sousa.

One day, a neighbour of ours – well, I call him neighbour not because we knew him, but because he lived in the same street (which, at the time, was still Rua Padre Sena Freitas) – went mad. He was a young man in his twenties who was said to have lost his wits by reading and studying too much. Just like Don Quixote. I remember one attack he had, the only one we actually witnessed, for afterwards we heard nothing more of him and presumed that he had been interned in Rilhafoles, the local insane asylum. Anyway, on that day, we – my mother, Conceição and I – heard terrible, heartrending cries coming from outside and ran to the window to find out what was going on. He lived on the top floor of a much taller building than ours, on the other side of the road and slightly to the right of the house we lived in, on the corner of Rua Cesário Verde. We saw him appear at the window again and again, as if he were intending to throw himself out, the proof of which was that two hands immediately appeared behind him, tugging at him, while he struggled and cried out over and over, in the most pitiful way: 'Ay, Santo Hilário! Ay, Santo Hilário!' Why he was calling on Santo Hilário we never found out. Shortly afterwards, an ambulance arrived, he was bundled inside and never came back, not at least during the time we lived there.

By then, I was already studying at technical college, the Escola Industrial de Afonso Domingues, in Xabregas, after two short years at secondary school, the Liceu Gil Vicente, which in those days was part of the São Vicente de Fora monastery. Here follows a chronology of my brief career as a student: I entered secondary school in 1933, when I was still only ten (classes started in October and my birthday falls in November), I was there during the school terms of 1933–1934 and 1934–1935, and I left to go to the technical college when I was coming up to thirteen. Of course, since technical subjects like Trade Skills, Mechanics and Mechanical Design form no part of the normal secondary school curriculum, I was in the first year for those subjects and the second year for everything else. So the sequence of my career there was as follows: 35–36, second and first year; 36–37, third and second; 37–38, fourth and third, 38–39, fifth and fourth, 39–40, fifth. The excursion to Sameiro – the one where I rode the horse that ignored me when I got off – took place at the end of 38–39 school year, just before the exams, and during that trip, I had the misfortune to twist my left foot jumping over something, cracking my heel bone in the process. As a result, I had to spend more than a month with a plaster cast up to my knee. There was a curved metal bar on the bottom of the cast, the ends of which were embedded in the plaster, and this was called a stirrup. That plaster boot was elaborately decorated with signatures, drawings and doodles by my fellow students. One of them suggested using it as a crib in the maths exam: 'Just pull up your trouser leg and bob's your uncle.' I managed to pass the exam without following his advice.

I think the time has come for me to tell you about another episode related to my arrival in the world. As if the delicate identity problem provoked by my surname wasn't enough, there was a further problem with the date of my birth. I was born on 16 November 1922, at two o'clock in the afternoon, and not on 18 November as the register of births, marriages and deaths would have it. My father was working away from home at the time and so not only was he unable to be present at his son's birth, the earliest he could get back was shortly after 16 December, probably the 17th, which was a

Sunday. Then, and I imagine now as well, a child's birth had to be registered within thirty days or you had to pay a fine. In those patriarchal times, and given that it was a legitimate birth, it would never have occurred to anyone that my mother or some other relative could go to the registry office, and given that the father of a child was officially considered to be the new-born's sole progenitor (on my enrolment card for secondary school, only my father's name appears, not my mother's), we waited for his return, and so as not to have to cough up for the fine (any amount, however small, would have been too much for the family's pocket), two days were added to my actual date of birth, and the problem was solved. Life in Azinhaga being what it was, painful and difficult, men would often go away to work for weeks on end, which is why I couldn't have been the first or the last example of such minor deceits. When I die, I will be two days older than the birthdate on my identity card, but I hope no one will notice.

Living to our right on the same floor (we had not yet left Rua Padre Sena Freitas) was a family comprising a couple and their young son. The husband worked as a painter at the Viúva Lamego ceramics factory in Largo do Intendente. The wife was Spanish, although I don't know from which part of Spain, and her name was Carmen, and their son, a fair-haired little boy, would have been about three (that's how I still remember him, as if he had never grown during all the time we lived there). We were good friends, the husband and I, which must seem surprising, given that he was an adult, practising a profession unusual in my tiny world, and I was just an awkward adolescent, full of doubts and certainties, although unaware of either. His surname was Chaves, I can't remember his first name or perhaps I never knew it, and so for me he was always and only Senhor Chaves. To keep ahead of his work or possibly to earn extra money, he would often work late at home, and that was when I used to visit him. I would knock on the door, his wife would open it – she was always very brusque and barely took any notice of me – and I would go through to the little dining-room where there stood, in one corner, lit by a reading lamp, the potter's wheel at which he worked. The high stool on which I always sat was there waiting for me. I used to enjoy watching him painting the already glazed ceramics with an almost grey paint which, after firing, would become the familiar blue of that particular type of pottery. And as the flowers, volutes, arabesques and scrolls flowed from his brushes we would talk. I may have been young and with, as you can imagine, limited experience of life, but I sensed that this sensitive, refined man was lonely. Today, I'm sure of this. I continued to visit him even when my family moved to Rua Carlos Ribeiro, and one day, I took him a few lines of popular verse I had written and which he then transferred onto a little heart-shaped dish whose intended recipient was Ilda Reis, with whom I had just started going out. If my memory serves me right, that must have been my first 'poetic composition', rather belated, it must be said, when you consider that I was almost eighteen or had already turned eighteen. Chaves was lavish with his praise and thought I should enter it in the *jogos florais*, as the delightful poetry contests much in vogue at the time were known and whose very innocence saved them from seeming ridiculous. The fruit of my poetic inspiration read thus: 'Careful, now, lest someone hear/The secret I unfold:/I give to you a china heart/for my heart you already hold.' You must admit that I would have deserved, at the very least, second prize...

The couple did not appear to get on very well, and his unpleasant Spanish wife found everything about Portugal detestable. While he was patient and refined, discreet and measured in his speech, she was the *guardia civil* type, tall and surly and rather broad in the beam, with a way with words that pitilessly garbled the language of Camões. That wouldn't have mattered so much if she hadn't been so aggressive. It was in their house that I first started listening to Radio Sevilla after the Spanish Civil War had begun. Oddly enough, given that she was Spanish, I never found out for certain which side they supported. I suspect, however, that Doña Carmen had sided with Franco from the start. Listening to Radio

Sevilla, I got into a terrible mental twist from which it took me a long time to free myself. The Nationalist General Queipo de Llano used the station to make his propaganda broadcasts, of which, needless to say, I remember not a word. What did stick in my memory was the jingle that always followed and which went: 'If lovely colours make you sing, Revi paints are just the thing.' There would be nothing very special about this if it weren't for the fact that I had become convinced that it was General Queipo de Llano himself who recited this jolly advertisement as soon as his broadcast was over. A necessary addendum to the 'minor matter' of the Spanish Civil War. Forgive my frivolity. More serious was my throwing out with the rubbish, a few months later, the map of Spain in which I had been sticking pins to mark the advances and retreats of the armies of both sides. It goes without saying that my sole source of information was the censored Portuguese press, which, like Radio Seville, never reported a Republican victory.

Leandro wasn't the only one to suffer the occasional bout of dyslexia or whatever it was. For example, I insisted that the word '*sacerdote*' – 'priest' – should be pronounced '*saquerdote*', but since, at the same time, I suspected that I must be wrong, if ever I had to say the word (given that it was such an 'erudite' word, this can't have happened very often and would happen even less today, when there are so few priests), I would always find a way of mumbling the word so that no one would have to correct me. I must have been the inventor of the so-called benefit of the doubt. After a while, I managed to resolve the difficulty by myself, and the word once again emerged as it should from my mouth. Another word I had problems with (these stories date from primary school days) was '*sacavenense*'. As well as meaning a native of the town of Sacavem, which has now been swallowed up by the insatiable dragon that Lisbon has become, it was also the name of a football club that may or may not have survived the vicissitudes of time and the purgatories of the second and third divisions. And how did I pronounce it then? In a truly shocking way that scandalised all who heard me: '*sacanavense*', which incorporated into the innocent original the word '*sacana*' with its echoes of libertinism and masturbation. I can still recall my relief when I was finally able to transpose the ill-bred syllables.

I must return once again to Rua dos Cavaleiros. The back of our house gave onto Rua da Guia, once known as Rua Suja – Grub Street – that joined another famous street, Rua do Capelão, which – accompanied inevitably by a guitar and several glasses of brandy – was always a fateful and unavoidable presence in fado songs and in any reminiscences about that first singer of fados, Maria Severa, and her fictional lover, the Marquis de Marialva. We had a view of the castle too, which is why I remember so vividly those shots whistling over our roof. We lived on the top floor (we almost always lived on the top floor because the rent was cheaper) in a room with use of kitchen, as the advertisements would inform us. There was no mention of a bathroom because such luxuries simply didn't exist, just a drain in one corner of the kitchen, open to the elements shall we say, which was intended for all manner of slops, both solid and liquid. At one point in my novel *The Manual of Painting and Calligraphy*, I write about the women who used to carry to the aforesaid drain the receptacles used for all nocturnal and diurnal deposits and which were usually covered by an immaculate white cloth and called '*bacios*' – 'chamber pots' – or, more rarely, '*penicos*' – 'pos' – perhaps because the latter was considered too plebeian by the families who used them. *Bacio* was more refined. I associate the house in Rua dos Cavaleiros and its steep, narrow stairs with the nightmares that afflicted me while asleep and awake, for as soon as night fell, every corner would fill up with shadows from which monsters would reach out to me with great clawed hands, terrifying me with their diabolical grimaces. I remember sleeping on the floor in my parents' room (there was, as I said, only one) and calling out to them, shaking with fear, because underneath the bed or inside an overcoat hanging from the hook or within the distorted shape of a chest of drawers or a chair, indescribable beings were stirring and threatening to leap out at me and devour me. The main source of these terrors was, I believe, that famous fleapit cinema in the Mouraria district, where, with my friend Félix, I received spiritual nourishment from the thousand faces of Lon Chaney, from wicked, cynical people of the very worst kind, from ghostly visions, supernatural magic, accursèd towers, dark underground passageways and from the whole paraphernalia, still in its infancy then, of cut-price collective and individual fear. In one such film, the leading man (that was what he was called in those days, although we denizens of the Fleapit referred to him unceremoniously as 'the guy') was seated romantically on a balcony, his right arm resting on the balustrade, and, to judge by the expression on his face, he was thinking of his beloved. Then, after a moment of suspense, a sinister, hooded leper began to climb towards him with agonising slowness, finally placing one of his disease-ridden hands on the pure white hand of the actor, who, straight away, before our very eyes, contracted Hansen's disease. Never in the history of human illness can there have been such a rapid case of contagion. The result of this horror was that, on that same night, when I was sleeping in the same bed as Félix (I don't know why, since it wasn't usual), I woke up in the dark and saw, in the middle of the room that also served as the other family's dining room, the leper from the film, exactly as he had appeared to us, all in black, with a pointed hood and a tall staff that came up to head height. I shook Félix awake and whispered in his ear: 'Look over there.' Félix looked and, explain it how you will, he saw exactly what I was seeing: a leper. Terrified, we pulled the blankets up over our heads and lay there for a long time, suffocating from fear and lack of air, until we dared to peer out over the edge of the sheet to find, with infinite relief, that the poor creature had vanished. At the end of the film, 'the guy' was cured by the faith that led him to bathe in the grotto at Lourdes, where he entered the water unclean and emerged pristine into the arms of the ingénue, or 'the girl', as we equally disrespectfully referred to her. These terrors came to an end when we moved to Rua Fernão Lopes, where a new fear – of dogs this time – awaited me. Our home in Rua dos Cavaleiros had been an attic room as it would be in Rua Fernão Lopes. When I looked out the back, the building seemed extraordinarily high, and later, even as an adult, I would often dream that I was falling from there, although the verb 'fall' should not be taken literally, that is, in the sense of plummeting helplessly earthwards, because what actually happened was that I would drift downwards, slowly brushing past the balconies on the lower floors, with their washing hung out to dry and their flower pots, and alight gently and unscathed on the cobblestones of Rua da Guia. Another very vivid memory from those days is of being despatched by my mother to buy salt from the grocer's opposite, and then, as I was coming back up the stairs, of opening the paper cone it was wrapped in and placing on my tongue just a few grains, which, as they dissolved, tasted at once strange and familiar. I also discovered the most primitive of drinks ever to pass my lips: a mixture of water, vinegar and sugar, the same mixture that I would use, albeit without the sugar, to slake Jesus' thirst in my novel *The Gospel According to Jesus Christ*. It was then, too, that I began training myself in 'artistic' drawing. I learned to draw a stork and an ocean liner, always the same way, a perfection I repeated over and over which is why, perhaps, I eventually tired of it. From then on, I became incapable of drawing anything, except, out of duty, the engine parts I had to tackle years later at technical college (drawing a cross-section of a carburettor, for example, was a task more suited to the perspicacity of a Sherlock Holmes than to the limited deductive powers of a fourteen-year-old). The person who taught me how to draw the ocean liner and the stork was Félix's father, who, I've just remembered, had very particular ideas about the best methods of applied pedagogy: he used to tie his son's ankle to the table leg with sewing thread and leave him there for as long as it took him to do his schoolwork. I hadn't yet started school then, but I accompanied Félix in his shame and wondered if one day my parents would do the same to me.

It wasn't all nasty shocks at the cinemas that let in boys, like me, with short trousers and close-cropped hair. There were comic cuts too, usually starring Charlie Chaplin, Buster Keaton, Laurel and Hardy, but the actors I liked best were Long & Short, who seem to have been completely forgotten. No one writes about them and their films don't appear on television. I used to see them mostly at the Cinema Animatógrafo, in Rua do Arco do Bandeira, where I used to go occasionally, and I remember how I laughed at a film in which they were pretending to be millers (I can see them now). Much later, I learned that they were Danish and that the tall, thin one was called Carl Schenstrom and the short, fat one Harald Madsen. Given their physical characteristics, it was inevitable that they would one day play Don Quixote and Sancho Panza respectively. That day came in 1926, but I never saw the film. The person I didn't like was Harold Lloyd. And I still don't.

I haven't yet spoken about my paternal grandparents. As the poet Murilo Mendes used to say of hell, they existed, but were not in good working order. He was João de Sousa and she was Carolina da Conceição, and they were not in the least affectionate, although it's true that they and I had few opportunities to find out how disposed we might be to displays of mutual affection. I saw them only rarely and found their apparent coldness towards me intimidating. This was a set of circumstances that I could clearly do nothing to make either better or worse, and so it seemed only natural that my safe haven in Azinhaga should have been the house of my maternal grandparents, as well as that of Aunt Maria Elvira in Mouchão de Baixo. Besides, Grandmother Carolina was never a particularly warm person. For example, I can't remember her ever giving me a kiss, or if she did, it was only a peck on the cheek (the difference is obvious), and I reckon that if she wasn't going to kiss me properly, it would have been better not to have bothered at all. The person who definitely disapproved of my evident preference for my maternal grandparents was my father, who curtly corrected me one day when I spoke of 'my grandparents', meaning my mother's parents, and he made no attempt to conceal his resentment, saying: 'You do have other grandparents.' What was I supposed to do? Pretend a love I didn't feel? Feelings can't be controlled, you can't just put them on or take them off when convenient, still less if the heart in question is a young heart and therefore guileless and pure. Grandmother Carolina died when I was ten. My mother turned up one morning at the school in Largo do Leão to bring the unfortunate news. She had come to fetch me, perhaps following some social convention of which I knew nothing, but which, apparently, on the death of a grandparent, required the grandchildren to be brought home at once. I remember glancing up at the clock on the wall in the entrance hall above the door, and thinking, like someone making a conscious effort to collect information that might prove useful to him in future, that I should make a note of the time. I seem to recall that it was a few minutes past ten. It appears that my pure and guileless heart had, in the end, decided to play the part of the cool observer subordinating emotion to the objective recording of the facts. The proof of this came with a second and still less pure and guileless thought, namely, that it would be a good idea to shed a few tears so as not to seem like a heartless grandchild in the eyes of my mother and the headmaster, Senhor Vairinho. I do remember that Grandmother Carolina had been very ill and had stayed at our house for some weeks. The bed she occupied was my parents' bed, and I have no idea where they slept during all that time. As for me, I slept in another room in the part of the house we were living in, on the floor with the cockroaches (I'm not inventing this, they used to scamper across me during the night). I remember hearing my parents using a word I thought must be the name of the illness my grandmother was suffering from: albumin (I realise now that she must have been suffering from albuminuria, but I wasn't that far out, since without albumin you can't have albuminuria). My mother used to treat her with warm vinegar poultices, although I don't know why. For a long time, the smell of warm vinegar remained associated in my memory with Grandmother Carolina.

Sometimes I wonder if certain memories are really mine or if they're just someone else's memories of episodes in which I was merely an unwitting actor and which I found out about later when they were told to me by others who had been there, unless, of course, they, too, had only heard the story from someone else. This is not the case with the little private school on the fourth or fifth floor of a building in Rua Morais Soares, where, before we went to live in Rua dos Cavaleiros, I started learning my alphabet. Seated on a low chair, I would trace the letters slowly and carefully on my slate, which I called '*pedra*' – 'stone' – because the proper term '*ardósia*' was too pretentious a word to emerge naturally from the mouth of a child, indeed, I may not even have known it at the time. This is a real, personal memory, picture perfect, complete with the satchel made from brown sacking with a piece of string attached so that I could wear it over my shoulder. I used to write on the slate with a slate pencil that you could buy in a stationer's and of which there were two types: one, the cheapest, was as hard as the slate you wrote on, while the other, more expensive, was smooth and soft, and we called it a 'milk pencil' because of its colour, a light milky grey. Only when I entered the official school system, and even then not during the first few months, did my fingers finally touch the small marvel of more up-to-date writing implements.

I don't know how children perceive time now, but as a child in those far-off days, time seemed to be made up of a particular kind of hour, each one of which was slow, dragging, interminable. A few more years had to pass before we began to understand, as we had to, that each hour had only sixty minutes and, later still, we would learn that every minute, without exception, ended after sixty seconds.

A photograph (now, alas, lost) was taken of me and my mother during the time when we lived in Rua Sabino de Sousa, in the Lisbon district of Alto do Pina. It showed my mother sitting on a bench outside a grocer's shop and me standing up, leaning back against her knees, with, beside us, a sack of potatoes bearing a hand-painted sign, as was the custom then in local shops and for many years afterwards as a way of telling customers how much something cost before they went into the shop: 50 *escudos* or five *tostões* a kilo. I must have been about three then and that would have been the oldest photo taken of me. I still have a baby photo of Francisco, the brother who died of bronchial pneumonia at four years old, in December 1924. I have occasionally thought that I could claim it as a photo of myself and thus enrich my personal iconography, but I never have. And it would be the easiest thing in the world given that, with my parents dead, there would no one to gainsay me, but stealing the image of someone who had already lost his life always seemed to me to show an unforgivable lack of respect, to be an inexcusable indignity. Render unto Caesar what is Caesar's, and to Francisco what could only belong to Francisco.

But to return to my village family, it was said that when he was born, Grandfather Jerónimo was placed on the foundling wheel of the poorhouse in Santarém, and there can be no doubt that he was, for Grandmother Josefa herself sometimes spoke of it, although without going into any detail, either because that was all she knew or because she preferred not to say too much. I knew even less about the circumstances surrounding the birth and life of his sister, my hated great-aunt Beatriz. Mentioning her was like mentioning rope in the house of a hanged man. The most intriguing question of all appears on my mother's birth certificate, which states that she was the grand-daughter of an unknown grandfather and of Beatriz Maria. Who was *she*? I haven't the faintest idea, but the coincidence of the name would, at the very least, be another element indicating that Jerónimo's mother must also have been the mother of Beatriz who lived next door. Great-aunt Beatriz's birth certificate, if it existed, would clear the matter up once and for all. But there's another strange aspect to this whole story. How could someone be recorded as unknown when he lived in a village where he couldn't help but be known? It's clear that Grandfather Jerónimo's mother either didn't want to or couldn't keep the child, which is why she placed him on the foundling wheel, but that still doesn't tell me what happened to the daughter Beatriz. Would she have been placed as a foundling too? It would seem that my famous Berber (or rather Moorish) great-grandfather – whose reputation as a breaker of hearts and feller of men reached my ears thanks to confidences vouchsafed to me by Grandmother Josefa – must have made great-grandmother Beatriz Maria pregnant twice, unless – and this would simplify everything – the brother and sister were twins, despite their obvious differences, he being tall and she short. One thing that never deceived anyone were the similarities (dark skin, sharp features, small, narrow eyes) that made Grandfather Jerónimo and his sister, my mother and all her siblings – Maria Elvira, Carlos, Manuel, Maria da Luz – easily identifiable as members of the same tribe. The male line that produced them clearly wasn't from the Ribatejo region. Contrary to what you might think, the Moorish great-grandfather, of whose sojourn in Azinhaga there appears to be not a scrap of written evidence, was not a romantic invention on my part in order to adorn my very modest family tree, but a clear genetic reality. He lived outside the village, in a hut among the willows, and he had two enormous dogs that used to frighten away any visitors by staring at them in silence and continuing to do so until they left. My Grandmother Josefa told me that one such visitor died and was buried right there. He had gone there to demand satisfaction from the Moor after the latter had seduced his wife (that was the polite way of putting it) and received in his chest the full blast of the Moor's hunting gun. No record has been found of the murderer having been tried for his crime. Who was he?

Equally real, and very hard, was the tumble I took on Avenida Casal Ribeiro, just round the corner from Rua Fernão Lopes, on a day that should have been a propitious one for human charity and for celestial benevolence, since the saint being celebrated was St Anthony, the defender of just causes and protector par excellence of things lost, no matter where. Unless (another hypothesis worth considering) my violent fall was an act of petty revenge on the part of that same holy personage when he noticed that the coins I was begging from passers-by were being used to buy sweets and, therefore, to satisfy the sin of greed, rather than as a contribution to the little altar, set up at the front door, as a lure for all good souls, believers and non-believers. The sad facts are these: in competition with my neighbourhood chums, I was intoning the usual cry: 'A penny for St Anthony, a penny for St Anthony' when I saw, passing by on the other side of Avenida Casal Ribeiro, a gentleman of advanced years, all dressed in black, wearing a hat and carrying a walking stick – a not uncommon sight in the streets of Lisbon in those primitive times. Anyway, before you could say 'Amen', I had spotted him and raced across the road, to get ahead of my competitors engaged in reaping the same harvest. The avenue was under repair, the road had been dug up (they were, I think, replacing the old, irregular basalt cobbles with tarmac), and the ground was covered in a kind of coarse gritty rubble that would have taken the skin off a crocodile. Anyway, I stumbled, fell on one knee, and when I did finally manage to get up, with blood pouring down my leg, the elderly gentleman merely gave me a glance of feigned compassion and continued on his way, thinking perhaps of his own dear grandchildren, so different from ill-bred urchins like me. Reduced to tears by the pain from my knee as well as the humiliation of having fallen at the feet of someone who had made not the slightest attempt to help me up, I dragged myself home, where my mother applied the inevitable iodine ointment and a bandage so tight that I couldn't bend my knee for several days. It's quite possible, now I think of it, that this unfortunate incident could have been the reason for me abandoning my incipient religious education. Living in the same building as us – in the second-floor apartment on the left if I'm not mistaken – was a very Catholic family (father, mother, son and daughter), and the lady of the house persuaded my mother to allow them to initiate me into the secrets of the Church in general and of the eucharist in particular. In short, they wanted to take me to Mass. My mother said Yes, ma'am and was duly grateful that such pleasant and distinguished neighbours should take an interest in her son, but, knowing her as I came to know her – a sceptic out of sheer indifference, except in the latter part of her life, when, as a widow, she started going to church with her friends in the area – I think she would have agreed just as readily to letting those or other neighbours take me to the beach. My problem now is whether this occurred before or after the fall. Whatever the sequence of events, and despite their sitting me down with them in the front pew, the two or three times I attended church proved most unpromising. When the sacristan rang the bell and the congregation obediently bowed their heads, I couldn't resist turning my head slightly to sneak a look at whatever it was we weren't supposed to see. Returning to the matter of my fall, though, if it happened before those church visits, this would mean that when they took me to Mass, I was already suspicious, disappointed with one saint and ready to believe that all the others were the same. If it happened afterwards, then my tumble could be taken as a punishment for having abandoned the true path that would lead me to paradise, in which case God would have behaved disgracefully, like a bullying bigot doling out a brutal punishment for a very minor offence and taking no account of my condition as young pagan or of my very brief Christian apprenticeship. I will never know. I must not forget, however, that at least once, the celestial powers did watch over me and two of my friends who also lived in Rua Fernão Lopes. I had come across a cartridge at home, quite how I can't remember, and carried it off to show my pals, but I didn't stop at just showing it to them. Instead, trembling with excitement, like conspirators, we gathered on some nearby steps and opened it in order to extract its innards, the gunpowder and the lead pellets. Crouched on the stone steps in the hallway, we held a match to the little pile of gunpowder to see what would happen. The ensuing deflagration was a modest one, but enough to give us a real fright. The only reason we didn't get our hands and faces burned was doubtless because St Anthony, or one of his many colleagues in the empyrean, interposed his providential, miracle-working hand between us and the explosion. A grazed knee was nothing in comparison.

When it occurred to me to describe that fall in Avenida Casal Ribeiro, I had in mind a photograph of myself and Aunt Maria Natália, taken by a street photographer in Parque Eduardo VII, where, every Sunday without fail, the maids from all the rich houses and the soldiers from all of Lisbon's barracks would go for a stroll. In that photograph, which has been lost along with so many others, I was wearing a shirt, short trousers and black knee-high socks held up by white elastic garters. A basic rule in the art of being smartly dressed requires that you should fold over the top of your sock to hide the garter, but I had not yet, it seems, been instructed in the finer points. In the photo, you could clearly see a scab on my left knee. This, however, dated not from my fall in Avenida Casal Ribeiro, but from a few years later, when I fell over in the playground at the Liceu Gil Vicente, and the gash had to be treated at the doctor's. They applied what they used to call a '*gato*', a small metal clamp used to hold the edges of the wound together and thus speed the healing process. The mark it left behind remained visible for years, and even now there's still a faint trace. Another scar I still have is the fine line of a razor cut, acquired one day in Mouchão do Baixo, when I was carving a boat out of a piece of cork. I was using the point of the blade to cut out lumps of cork so as to make what would be the inside of the boat, when, suddenly, due to a weak spring, the razor snapped shut and the blade cut through the first thing it found in its path, namely, the outer edge of my right index finger, by the side of my nail. It very nearly took with it a slice of my flesh. I was treated with one of the miraculous remedies of the day, alcohol and balsam. The wound didn't become infected and healed perfectly. Aunt Maria Elvira always said that I was made of good solid stuff.

Aunt Maria Natália worked as a maid in the Formigal household (the master and mistress were usually referred to in the plural as the Senhores Formigais), along with an outside maid, who was the one who did the shopping and ran other errands. I remember one morning (I'd perhaps gone there to collect my aunt for our fortnightly Sunday walk) standing in the kitchen (I'd never seen anything like it and so was fascinated by the black oven, the little doors of varying sizes with their gleaming copper frames, and the boiler always full of hot water) when old Senhor Formigal came in, accompanied by his wife, Dona Albertina, who was equally advanced in years, but still a fine-looking woman. The cook and the two maids, inside and outside, curtsied and lined up, awaiting their orders, but Senhor Formigal, who wore a goatee and a moustache as white as the hair on his head, had only come to inspect (out of politeness, not because he was a doctor or a nurse) the knee I had split open in Avenida Casal Ribeiro. He regarded me with an understanding, protective air and asked: 'So you hurt your patella, did you?' I will never forget that word. I had hurt my knee, not my patella, but he must have felt that 'knee' was too vulgar a term, unworthy of his person. I looked down at my battered joint, and all I could say was: 'Yes, sir.' He patted my cheek and left, followed by Dona Albertina. Aunt Maria Natália glowed with pride, while the cook and the outside maid looked at me as if a heavenly halo were encircling my head, as if hitherto unsuspected qualities had bloomed in the inside maid's otherwise insignificant nephew, qualities that the white, manicured hand of Senhor Formigal, when he lightly touched my cheek and my close-cropped hair, had finally caused to spring into life. The Senhores Formigais were about to go out, probably to Mass, but Dona Albertina returned to the kitchen in order to give me a little bag of chocolates: 'Here, these are for you, to help your knee get better faster,' she said and was gone, leaving behind her a whiff of face-powder and having put that word 'patella' firmly in its place. I don't know if it was then that my aunt took me to see their bedroom – I think not – but it was a magnificent, solemn, almost ecclesiastical room, all adorned with scarlet draperies, the canopy, the coverlet, the plump pillows, the bed curtains, the upholstery on the chairs: 'It's all done in the very best, the very finest damask,' my aunt told me, and when I asked her why they had that S-shaped sofa at the end of the bed, she replied: 'That's a love seat, he sits on one side and she on the other, so that they can talk without having to turn their heads, it's very practical.' Since we were there, I would have liked to try it out, but my aunt wouldn't even let me across the threshold. The chocolates and I met with far worse luck later on. I ate a few before leaving the Formigais' house, and they left in my mouth a foretaste of paradise, but my aunt was categorical on the matter: 'Don't eat any more, they'll make you sick', and I, being a good little boy, obeyed. Since I have no memory of strolling through Parque Eduardo VII with a bag of chocolates in my hand, especially since I was forbidden to eat them, we must have gone straight from there to Rua Fernão Lopes, where my aunt deposited me, having first described, in, I imagine, lavish detail, the episode in the kitchen, the kindness her employers had shown to me, Senhor Formigal patting my cheek and the chocolates given to me by the lady of the house, so very kind. Darkness fell, and, since at the time we had no radio on which we could listen to songs from the latest shows, we kept the same hours as the chickens, and so my mother soon packed me off to bed. My parents and I slept in the same room, they in the double bed and I on a small divan, almost a camp-bed really, underneath the sloping roof. On the other side of the room, on a chair standing against the wall, stood the longed-for bag of chocolates. When my mother and father came to bed, first, my father, as usual, then my mother, because there were always dishes to wash or socks to darn, I had my eyes closed, pretending to sleep. They turned out the light and fell asleep, but I couldn't settle. Later, with the room in darkness, I slowly got up, tiptoed over to get the bag of chocolates and, in three furtive steps, crept back into bed where I snuggled happily down between the sheets to gorge myself until I slipped into unconsciousness. When I woke the next day, I found, squashed beneath me, what remained of my night feast, a sticky, soft, brown chocolate paste, the dirtiest, most repellent thing my eyes had ever seen. I wept bitter tears of vexation, and tears of embarrassment and frustration too, which was perhaps why my parents didn't punish or scold me. I was unhappy enough as it was. I had given in to the sin of greed, and greed was punishing me with no need for sticks or stones.

On the occasional Sunday afternoon, the women would go down to the Baixa to window-shop. They usually walked there, but sometimes took the tram, which was the worst thing that could happen to me at that age, because I soon grew queasy from the smell inside; the overheated, almost fetid atmosphere set my stomach churning and within minutes I would be throwing up. In that respect, I was a delicate child. With the passing of time that olfactory intolerance (I don't know what else

85

to call it really) diminished, but for years afterwards, I only had to board a tram for my head to start to swim. Anyway, on that particular Sunday, for whatever reason – whether because she felt sorry for me or simply wanted to stretch her legs – my mother, along with Conceição, Emilia too, I think, and me, decided to walk there from Rua Fernão Lopes, along Avenida Fontes Pereira de Melo, then down Avenida da Liberdade to the Chiado, which was where Ali Baba kept his most valued treasures. I don't remember the shop windows, and that isn't what I'm here to talk about. I'm concerned with more serious matters. Next to one of the doors to the department store, Armazéns Grandella, a man was selling balloons, and whether it was because I asked (which I doubt very much because only someone who expects to be given something will run the risk of asking) or because my mother, unusually, wanted to make a public demonstration of her love for me, one of those balloons ended up in my hands. I can't remember if it was green or red, yellow or blue, or simply white. What happened afterwards erased from my memory a colour that should have stayed in my eyes for ever, because that was neither more nor less than the first balloon I had been given in my six or seven years of life. We were walking across the Rossio, on our way home, and I was as proud as if I were dragging the whole world through the air tied to a piece of string, when, suddenly, I heard someone behind me snicker. I turned and I saw. The balloon had deflated and, without my realising, I had been dragging it along the ground – a grubby, shrivelled, shapeless thing – and two men were laughing and pointing at me. I felt, on that occasion, the most ridiculous of human beings. I didn't even cry. I simply dropped the string, grabbed my mother's arm like a drowning man a piece of wood and kept walking. That grubby, shrivelled, shapeless thing *was* the world.

One day, at around this time, I went on a trip to Mafra. I had been born in Azinhaga and was living in Lisbon, and there I was, possibly in response to a knowing look or an indecipherable wink from the fates, being taken to the place where, more than fifty years later, my future as a writer would be decided once and for all. I don't remember now if the Baratas came with us or not. I have a vague idea that we were driven there in the car of some acquaintance of my father's, who, as far as I know, left no other trace of his passage through our lives. My most vivid memory of that brief visit (we didn't go into the monastery, only the basilica) is of a statue of St Bartholomew which stood, as it still does, in the second chapel on the left as you go in, on the side which I believe is called, in liturgical language, the gospel side. A combination of extreme youth, a complete ignorance of the world of statues and the dim lighting in the chapel meant that I probably wouldn't even have noticed that poor St Bartholomew had been flayed had it not been for the guide's practised patter and his smugly eloquent gesture as he indicated the folds of flaccid skin (flaccid even though they were made of marble) that the poor martyr was holding in his hands. Dreadful. There is no mention of St Bartholomew in *Baltasar and Blimunda*, but it is quite possible that the memory of that awful moment was still lurking somewhere in my mind when, in 1980 or 1981, I once again gazed upon the vast bulk of the palace and the towers of the basilica and said to the people with me: 'One day, I'd like to put all this in a novel.' I can't swear to it, I'm just saying that it's possible.

Between the ages of two and four or five, I must have made quite a few journeys to Azinhaga in my mother's arms. My father had gone from being a vulgar digger of fields to public servant, a policeman no less, with a basketful of news and novelties from the city to recount, and it was most unlikely that he would have remained in Lisbon during his annual leave, when he could enjoy showing off to his former work colleagues, talking posh or at least trying hard not to sound too provincial and, in the intimacy of the tavern, after a couple of glasses of wine, regaling them with stories of women, a prostitute, say, who would pay with her body for a certain degree of police protection – not that he himself would admit to such things – or a market-trader of easy virtue in the Praça da Figueira. Many years later, my grandmother would tell me that, whenever I was left in her care, she would sit me in the next room, on a blanket spread on the floor, from where, after a while, she would hear me say: 'Gramma, gramma.' 'What's wrong, sweetheart?' she would ask. And I would reply tearfully, sucking my right thumb (was it my right thumb?): 'Want to poo.' By the time she had rushed to my aid, it was always too late. 'You were already all dirty,' she would say, laughing. My mother, Francisco and I had left for Lisbon in the spring of 1924, when I was, at most, eighteen months old, so my communicative skills weren't really up to much. Presumably, though, such scatological episodes must have taken place later, on those holiday visits to Azinhaga, when my mother, leaving me in the hands of Grandmother Josefa, would go off to catch up on the latest gossip with her childhood friends, to whom she would report on her own experiences of civilisation, including, if pride or shame did not tie her tongue, the frequent beatings she received from a husband disoriented by the erotic delights of the Lisbon metropolis. And perhaps it's because I was an astonished and frightened witness to some of those deplorable domestic scenes that I've never raised my hand to a woman. It served me as a vaccine.

This was a time when women would consult the local witch when things were going wrong at home. Even during the time we were living in Rua Fernão Lopes, I remember the prayers and smoke with which my mother would fill the room as she tossed some small, dark, round seeds onto the embers in the stove, all the while intoning a spell that began thus: '*Cocas, minhas cocas ...*' I can't remember how the rest of it went, but I can recall the smell of the seeds, so intense that even now I can feel it in my nose. They gave off a sickly smoke, simultaneously sweet and nauseating, that made you dizzy. I never found out what *cocas* were, but they must have been something oriental. Maybe that's why I still can't stand the stench from the joss-sticks with which people often contaminate their apartments in the belief that it makes them more spiritual.

One day, on a melon patch near Mouchão de Baixo, Aunt Maria Elvira, José Dinis and I – why I can't remember, although I'm sure it can't have been mere chance – met up with Alice and her parents, and my angry cousin, seeing that the girl was paying more attention to me than to him, was, inevitably, filled with such jealousy that he flung his slice of melon at me. He aimed it at my face, but missed and hit my shirt instead. As I said earlier, we were always like cat and dog, at each other's throats over the slightest thing. But it's Alice I'm interested in now. The moment has come to speak of her in more detail than I have up to now. Some time after this incident (I think it was the following summer), the three of us went to Vale de Cavalos, where her family had moved (they had lived in Alpiarça before), and if my memory serves me right, we even visited her house. (I can't be absolutely sure that things happened exactly in this sequence, but there was one occasion, presumably this one, when I learned the short cut from Mouchão de Baixo to Vale de Cavalos across the fields via footpaths and tracks.) Now it so happened that one or two weeks later, some festivities or other were being held in that village, and I decided that I absolutely had to see Alice. I was fifteen and this was the summer of the year in which I would turn sixteen. In the earlier pages of this book, I described certain somewhat romantic adventures, like crossing the Tejo, Graviel's boat coming in to shore, its bottom scraping over the tiny pebbles on the river bed, the crepuscular light, the long walk there and back. I won't, however, repeat them here, for now I must find the courage to turn the coin over and show you the other side. There was dancing in the village square and the local band was playing with an enthusiasm appropriate to the occasion. I talked to Alice, who seemed quite pleased to see me, although not overly so, and I danced with her (if you can call it dancing, for she took more of a lead than I did, and I have a suspicion – not to say certainty – that, at one point, she shot a look of quiet resignation at a girlfriend of hers who was dancing nearby). Finally, when it was getting late (it was that look, I realise now, that made me renounce Alice for ever), I gave up and said goodbye. Even today I wonder how I didn't get lost in the night full of noises and shadows, when only a few years before I had lived in fear and trembling of the darkness and the monsters it engenders. Towards the end of my long walk, I was so exhausted and my legs so weary that I took shelter in a rough straw-thatched, wattle-and-daub shack, which was, as I found out later, where Uncle Francisco Dinis used to rest occasionally on his night patrols of the estate. Starving hungry, I groped around inside for something to eat and found only the aforementioned piece of cornbread, a stale and mouldy piece as I discovered in the morning when I ate what was left of it. There was no mattress on the truckle bed, but the layer of corn husks on which I stretched out my weary body smelled good. I slept for what little remained of the small hours and, in the morning, my uncle appeared. I heard the barking of the dog that always accompanied him – Piloto his name was – and I emerged from the hut, still dazed with sleep and dazzled by the light. When I reached Mouchão de Baixo, I recounted my adventures to Aunt Maria Elvira and José Dinis, to the great despair of the latter, because I took the precaution of omitting any hint of the humiliation I had suffered at my romantic failure. Alice had wanted me to lead her in the dance, and I hadn't known how. The tailor had more luck. It would be interesting to know, although we never will, if she was as lucky as him.

I was never much of a fisherman. Like any boy of my age and modest means, I used an ordinary rod with a hook, sinker and cork float tied to the fishing line, nothing that remotely resembled the modern artefacts that would appear later on and which I saw in the hands of certain local amateurs when I was already grown up and had abandoned my piscatorial dreams. Consequently, I never caught anything more than a few small carp, a young barbel (very rarely), and many hours spent in vain (well, none were spent in vain, because, without my realising it, I was 'fishing' for things that would be just as important for me in the future, images, smells, sounds, soft breezes, sensations). In the sun, if it wasn't too fierce, or in the shade of a weeping willow, waiting for a fish to bite. Seated at the water's edge, I usually fished in 'our village's river', the Almonda, in the late afternoon, because when the weather was too hot, the fish disappeared into their hiding places on the riverbed and wouldn't take the bait. At other times, I would sit on one side or other of the river mouth or, on a few notable occasions, would row farther off, across to the south bank of the Tejo and stay there, in the shelter of a brake of trees as if under a canopy, and that was what I liked best. The local fishermen emeriti would boast of having their own methods, their own strategies, their own magical arts, which usually lasted for a season and then gave way to other methods, strategies and magical arts that were always better than the previous ones. I never found any of them useful. The only one I can remember was a special rose dust (I never knew at the time, and still don't know to this day, which part of the rose the cognoscenti pulverised: I assume it was the petals), thanks to which – once it had been thrown into the water like some kind of poetic bait – the fish would flock, if you'll forgive the inappropriate comparison, like pigeons to chaff. I, poor wretch, never touched that gold dust with my unworthy fingers. And that must explain my ill luck in catching, or failing to catch, the largest (although for ever invisible) barbel in the entire piscine history of the Tejo. I will describe very simply the whole regrettable affair. I had gone with my fishing tackle to the mouth – as we called it – of the Almonda, where, at the time, a narrow tongue of sand reached out into the Tejo, and there I was, with the day fading fast and not a twitch from the cork float to indicate any signs of subaquatic life, when, suddenly, without even having felt the initial exciting tremor that announces a fish trying to nibble the bait, the float plunged down into the depths, almost snatching the rod from my hands. I pulled and was pulled, but the struggle was short-lived. The line must have been badly secured or rotten, because with one violent tug, the fish carried everything off, hook, line and sinker. Imagine my despair. There, on the edge of the deep water into which the rascal had disappeared, I stood staring at the now calm surface, holding the ridiculous, useless rod in my hands, not knowing what to do next. That was when I had the most absurd idea of my entire life: I decided to run home, get another line, float and sinker for my rod and return to settle accounts once and for all with the monster. Now, my grandparents' house was just over half a mile from that spot, and you would have to be a complete idiot (either that or very innocent) to nurture the ludicrous hope that the barbel would wait there killing time, quietly digesting not only the bait, but the hook, line and sinker, not to mention the float, until the next titbit arrived. Despite this, and against all reason and good sense, I raced off along the river bank, took a short cut through olive groves and stubble fields, and burst, panting, into the house, where, while I prepared my rod, I told my grandmother what had happened, and she asked me if I really thought the fish would still be there, not that I heard her, I didn't want to, I couldn't. I returned to the spot, even though the sun had already set, I cast my hook into the water and waited. I don't think there is a deeper silence in the world than the silence of water. I felt it then and never forgot it. I stayed until I could barely see the float bobbing gently on the current, then, finally, with a heavy heart, I rolled up my line and returned home. That barbel had obviously lived a long time and must have been a large beast, but it certainly wouldn't end up dying of old age, someone else was bound to catch it one day. In a way, though, with my hook caught in its gills, it bore my mark, it was mine.

One day I was fishing in the Tejo estuary, for once in peace and harmony with José Dinis (I'm not sure that it really was the estuary, because we hadn't walked that far, nor in the right direction, to have come so close to the river; it was probably just a large pool, deep enough not to dry up in the searing summer heat and inhabited by a few colonies of fish that had arrived there with the flood waters), and we had already caught two scrawny specimens, when two boys, more or less our age, appeared, who must have been from Mouchão de Cima, which is why we didn't know them (nor would that have been advisable), even though we only lived a stone's throw away. They sat down behind us, and the usual conversation began: 'Had any bites?' and we said 'Oh, not too bad', reluctant to give them any information. In the end, so that they wouldn't make fun of us, we told them that we'd caught two fish and that they were in the pot. The 'pot' was a cylindrical tin with a tight lid and a wire handle that you could sling over your arm. These pots, usually slung from a pole carried over the shoulder, were used by the workers to carry their food to the fields, a thick tomato soup perhaps, if it was the season, or cabbage soup with beans, or whatever was within the means of each individual. Having made it clear that we weren't as green as we looked, we turned our attention to the floats sitting utterly still on the leaden surface of the water. A great silence fell, time passed, and after a while, one of us glanced behind and saw that the boys had gone. Our hearts fell when we opened the pot. Instead of the two fish, there were two twigs floating in the water. How the thieves managed, without making a sound, to take off the lid, remove the fish and escape is something I still don't understand. When we got home and described what had happened, Aunt Maria Elvira and Uncle Francisco roared with laughter. We could hardly blame them, it was all we deserved.

It must be said that I was even less skilled as a hunter than I was as a fisherman. Only one sparrow ever fell to my catapult, but I killed it so ineptly and in such sad circumstances that one day I had to ease my conscience and express my sorrow by recounting the vile deed in a story. However, while I may have been no marksman when it came to the birds of the air, the same was not true of the frogs of the Almonda, which I felled with a slingshot that was as accurate as it was pitiless. The truth is that children's cruelty knows no limits (which is the real reason why adult cruelty knows no bounds either): what harm had those innocent batrachians done to me as they sat taking the sun in the shifting mud, enjoying the warmth from above and the cool from beneath? The stone whistled towards them, hitting them full on, and the poor frogs gave their last leap and lay there, belly up. The river – more charitable than the perpetrator of those deaths – washed away the few drops of spilled blood, while I, triumphant and unaware of my own stupidity, went upstream and downstream in search of new victims.

It's odd that I've never heard anyone anywhere else mention the 'seamstress'. As the precocious rationalist I had already shown myself to be at a tender age (you need only recall the heretical episode at Mass, when the bell rang and I craned my neck to see what it was they didn't want me to see), I thought, and I think I even suggested as much to my mother, that it might just be woodworm or some other similar creature, a ridiculous idea because woodworm (which aren't really worms, but larvae) couldn't live inside the thick mortar used in buildings then, which was far too hard to chew, although not as hard as modern-day cement and concrete. So what was it then? In the silent house, my mother would always say at some point, as though it were the most natural thing in the world: 'There's the seamstress.' And I would press my ear to the place on the wall she had indicated and I could hear, I swear I could hear, the unmistakable sound of a sewing machine, the pedal-operated variety (there was no other kind then) and also, sometimes, another characteristic sound, slower, that of braking, when a seamstress raises her right hand to the wheel to stop the movement of the needle. I heard them in Lisbon, but also in Azinhaga, in my grandparents' house, where Grandmother Josefa or Aunt Maria Elvira would say: 'There's the seamstress, there she is again.' The sounds that emerged from the innocent blankness of the white-washed wall were just the same. The explanation I was given was quite fantastical – how could it not be? – namely, that what we were hearing was the sad consequence of an irreverent seamstress who had worked on a Sunday and been condemned for that grave fault (there was no information about the identity of the judge) to work at her sewing-machine for all eternity inside the walls of houses. This mania for mercilessly punishing any Christian who needed to work on a Sunday had claimed another victim in the distant past, or so they told me, the man in the moon, the man you can see so clearly from here below, with a bundle of firewood on his back, and who was placed there, shouldering that eternal load, to serve as a lesson to anyone rash enough to be tempted to follow his bad example. But to go back to the 'seamstress' in the walls, I don't know what can have happened in the world for her to have disappeared so completely, because it's over seventy years now since I last heard her and I can find no one else who has. Perhaps her sentence was commuted. If so, I hope the same mercy is shown to the man in the moon. The poor thing must be worn out. Besides, if they removed him from there, if they got rid of that shadow, the moon would give more light and we would all stand to gain.

As I've mentioned before, my grandparents' house was called Casalinho, and the name of the district was Divisões, perhaps because the rather sparse olive grove opposite (it became a football field later on and more recently still was turned into a park) had various owners, and each tree, as if they were cattle not trees, bore carved on the trunk its owner's initials. The house was of the very roughest construction, one storey high, although it was raised about three feet above the ground in case of flood, with no window on the blank frontage, just the traditional door with the hatch in it. There were two spacious rooms, the *casa-de-fora* – the outside room, so called because it gave onto the street – which was furnished with two beds and a few chests, three if my memory serves me right, and the kitchen, both rooms having only roof tiles above and a dirt floor beneath. At night, once the oil lamp had been turned out, you could see the occasional vagabond star twinkling through the chinks in the roof. At irregular intervals, perhaps every two or three months, my grandmother would re-surface the floor of the *casa-de-fora*. She would dissolve the requisite amount of mud in a bucket of water and then, on her knees, using a cloth soaked in the mixture, she would shuffle backwards, making sweeping movements with her arm and gradually covering the floor with a new layer. We were not allowed in until the mud had dried completely. I still have the smell of that damp mud in my nose and, in my eyes, the red of the floor growing gradually paler as the water evaporated. As I recall, the kitchen floor didn't receive the same treatment, it was swept, of course, although not much, but it never received that coating of mud. Apart from the beds and the chests, there was in the *casa-de-fora* a tall, unvarnished wooden table with an old mirror, tarnished and flawed, a mantel clock and a few other worthless knick-knacks. (Much later, long after I was forty, I bought in a Lisbon antique shop a similar clock, which I still have today, like something borrowed from my childhood.) The mirror was part of a small, rather inelegant dressing table, also unvarnished, with a central drawer and two small side drawers full of useless bits and pieces, and these contents remained unchanged, it seemed, from one year to the next. Photos of the family were gathered together on the table like a galaxy of faces; it never occurred to anyone to arrange them, like a decoration, on the whitewashed walls of the *casa-de-fora*. They were placed there like saints on an altar, like the disparate parts of a collective reliquary, fixed and immutable. The kitchen was the world. There were two beds, a table that wobbled on the uneven floor and so always had to have something jammed under one leg to keep it level, two blue-painted chairs, and the fireplace with, at the back, the 'fireplace doll', a blurred, vaguely anthropomorphic figure, which disappeared, along with everything else, when Uncle Manuel, the youngest of my maternal uncles and a policeman like my father, inherited the house after my grandmother died, only to build in its place a house that anyone with even average taste would have found hideous, but which he must have thought extraordinary. I never asked him if he was pleased with his work, because, in keeping with deep-seated family tradition, we were no longer on speaking terms. I imagine that the 'doll' was a rough representation of some pagan domestic genius, for example, one of the Roman penates (a common Portuguese expression of the day was '*regressar a penates*' which meant simply 'to go home'). As far as one could tell from the shape, it must have been made out of square bricks, two of which were stuck in the wall, side by side, to form the upper part of the trunk, with another placed on top of them in the centre as the neck and a third placed end on to represent the head. It was my grandmother who called it the 'fireplace doll', and that satisfied me until, years later, thanks to the cognitive virtues of reading, I thought I had discovered its true identity. Had I really? The fireplace was a small one, only large enough for two to sit round, usually my grandfather and myself. In winter, when the water froze in the jugs overnight and, in the morning, we had to break the ice with a stick, we would be burned to a crisp in front and shivering behind. When the cold gripped, there was very little difference between being inside or out. The kitchen door, which gave onto the yard, was extremely old and more like a gate than a door, with cracks in it big enough to put your hand through and, even more extraordinary, it had been like that for years and years. It seemed as if it must have been old already when it was hung on its hinges. Only later, once my grandfather Jerónimo had died (he departed this life in 1948), did it benefit from a few repairs or, rather, a little patching up. I don't think it was ever replaced though. It was to this most humble of homes that my grandparents came to live after they were married, she – or so people said at the time – the prettiest girl in Azinhaga and he, the foundling from the poorhouse in Santarém, whom people called '*pau-preto*' – 'blackwood' – because of his dark skin. And there they would live for ever. My grandmother told me that on their wedding night, Grandfather Jerónimo had sat outside the front door, armed with a big stick, waiting for the jealous rivals who had sworn to come and throw stones at the roof. No one came, though, and all night (if you'll allow me to give free rein to my imagination) the moon travelled across the sky, while my grandmother, lying in bed, eyes open, waited for her husband. And it was daylight before they could embrace.

The time has come to speak of the celebrated novel *Maria, the Fairy of the Forest*, which brought tears to the eyes of so many families in working-class areas of Lisbon in the 1920s. It was published, I believe, by Edições Romano Torres and distributed in weekly instalments or sixteen-page pamphlets, which were delivered on the same day each week to subscribers' homes. We, too, received it in our top-floor apartment in 57 Rua dos Cavaleiros, but, at that point, apart from a dim memory of tracing the letters of the alphabet on a slate, which was not that helpful, my initiation into the delicate art of deciphering hieroglyphics had not yet begun. The person charged with reading to us out loud, for my mother's and my edification, for we were both of us illiterate – as I would continue to be for some time and as my mother would remain for the rest of her life – was Félix's mother, whose name, however hard I try, I cannot recall. The three of us, reader and listeners, would sit on the inevitable low benches and allow ourselves to be carried on the wings of the word to that world so different from ours. I remember that among the many misfortunes which, over the weeks, rained down upon the head of poor Maria, a victim of the hatred and envy of a wicked and very powerful female rival, there was one episode that would remain for ever engraved on my memory. During one of her many adventures, which I have long since forgotten and which it would, besides, be of no interest to detail here, Maria had been imprisoned in the gloomy depths of her mortal enemy's castle, and her enemy – as if to confirm what we, the esteemed readers, already knew from previous episodes, namely, that she had been a nasty piece of work from the cradle up – was taking advantage of the fact that poor Maria was highly gifted in the arts of embroidery and other such feminine crafts and forcing her, under threat of the worst punishments known and unknown, to embroider and sew. She was, as you see, not only evil, but exploitative too. Now, among the many beautiful pieces that Maria had produced during the time of her imprisonment was a magnificent negligée, which the chatelaine had decided to reserve for her own use. Then, in one of those extraordinary coincidences that only occur in novels and without whose aid no novelist would ever bother to write one, the elegant gentleman who loved Maria and whose feelings were tenderly reciprocated came to visit that very castle, never imagining that his beloved was imprisoned there in a dungeon where she was ruining her white fingers by embroidering day and night. The chatelaine, who had long had her eye on him – he being the reason for the bitter rivalry between her and Maria – resolved to seduce him that very night. No sooner said than done. At dead of night, she slipped surreptitiously into her guest's bedroom, having donned said negligée and made herself provocative and perfumed enough to turn the heads of all the saints in the heavenly court, let alone an energetic gentleman in the prime of life, however in love he might be with the pure and long-suffering Maria. Indeed, as he lay in the arms of the immoral creature who had entered his bed, as he bent over the round, intoxicating breasts clearly evident beneath the lace, just as he was about to surrender and fall into the seductive abyss, just when the perfidious creature was about to cry victory, the gentleman recoiled as if he had been bitten by the asp hidden between Cleopatra's breasts, and, grasping the embroidery, cried out: 'Maria! Maria!' What could have happened? I know this will be hard to believe, but this is what the author wrote. In her prison, much as a shipwreck victim throws a bottle into the water in the hope that his message will be picked up by some saving hand, Maria had embroidered a cry for help on the negligée, complete with her name and the place where she was imprisoned. Saved from ignominy at the very last moment, the gentleman violently repelled the lubricious lady and raced off to rescue from captivity his virginal and adored Maria. It must have been around then that we moved to Rua Fernão Lopes, which is why *The Fairy of the Forest* had to finish there, because the subscription had been paid for by Félix's mother. We benefited from that weekly free reading, which was no small thing, especially as far as I was concerned, for even though I was very young at the time, I never forgot that dramatic and troubling episode.

It did not take me long to learn to read. Thanks to the training I had begun to receive in my first school, in Rua Martens Ferrão, of which I remember only the entrance and the dark stair, I moved on, almost seamlessly, to the regular study of advanced Portuguese in the form of a newspaper, the *Diário de Notícias*, which my father brought home with him every day and which I presume was given to him by a friend, a particularly thriving newsvendor perhaps or a tobacconist. I very much doubt that he would have bought it, for the very pertinent reason that we didn't have enough money to spend on such luxuries. To give you a clear idea of the situation, I need say only that for years, with absolute regularity, my mother used to pawn the blankets as soon as winter was over, only to retrieve them once the cold weather began to bite again and she had saved enough to pay back the monthly interest and the amount of the loan. Obviously I couldn't read that august daily newspaper fluently, but one thing was clear to me: the articles in the paper were written using the same characters (although we called them letters, not characters) whose names, functions and mutual relationships I was learning about in school. And so I was reading even before I could spell properly, even though I couldn't necessarily understand what I was reading. Being able to identify a word I knew was like finding a signpost on the road telling me I was on the right path, heading in the right direction. And so it was, in this rather unusual way, *Diário* by *Diário*, month by month, pretending not to hear the jokey comments made by the adults in the house, who were amused by the way I would stare at the newspaper as if at a wall, that my moment to astonish them finally came, when, one day, nervous but triumphant, I read out loud, in one go, without hesitation, several consecutive lines of print. I couldn't understand everything I was reading, but that didn't matter. Apart from my father and mother, the other adults present, once so sceptical and now so impressed, were the Baratas. In that house without books, it so happened that there was one fat book, bound, I believe, in sky-blue, and which was entitled *The Warbler of the Windmill*, whose author, if my memory serves me right, was Émile de Richebourg, a name that does not feature prominently in any histories of French literature, however detailed, if, indeed, it appears at all, and yet he was a master of the art of using the word to move sensitive souls and arouse the passions. The owner of this literary gem, which appeared to have been originally published in serial form, was Conceição Barata, who kept it like a treasure in a drawer in the dresser, wrapped in tissue paper and smelling of mothballs. This novel was to be my first great experience as a reader. I was still a long way from the municipal library in Palácio das Galveias, but my first step in that direction had been taken. And thanks to the fact that we and the Barata family lived together for a good two years, I had more than enough time to read to the end and start again. However, try how I might, I cannot, as I can with *Maria, the Fairy of the Forest*, remember a single passage from the book. Émile de Richebourg would be most offended by such a lack of respect, he who thought he had written his *Warbler* in indelible ink, but things did not stop there. Years later, I would discover, to my great surprise, that I had also read Molière in that sixth-floor apartment in Rua Fernão Lopes. One day, my father came home with a book (I can't imagine where he got it from) which was neither more nor less than a Portuguese–French guide to conversation, with the pages divided into three columns, the first, on the left, in Portuguese, the second, in the middle, in French, and the third, alongside that, indicating how to pronounce the words in the second column. Among the various situations in which a Portuguese speaker might need the guide's help to communicate in French (a railway station, a hotel reception, an office hiring out carriages, a port, a tailor's shop, buying tickets for the theatre, trying on a suit at the tailor's etc.) there suddenly appeared a dialogue between two men, one of whom seemed to be a teacher of sorts and the other some kind of pupil. I read it over and over because I so enjoyed the astonishment of the man who was unable to believe what the teacher was telling him, that he had been speaking prose since he was born. I knew nothing about Molière (how could I?), but I made a grand entrance into his world when I had barely got beyond knowing my vowels. No doubt about it, I was a lucky boy.

I cannot recall the first name of the headmaster at the school in Largo do Leão – to which I was transferred when I'd completed my first year in Rua Martens Ferrão – but I do remember that he had a strange surname, Vairinho (I can't find a single Vairinho in the current Lisbon telephone directory), and that he was a tall, thin man, with a severe face, who disguised his baldness by combing over the hair from one side of his head and gluing it down with brilliantine, just as my father used to do, although I must confess I found my teacher's hairstyle more presentable than my progenitor's. Even at such a tender age, I found my father's appearance slightly grotesque (if you'll forgive such disrespect), especially when I saw him get out of bed with those scant locks of hair hanging down on the side that was natural to them and revealing the bare, pale cranium, because as a policeman, of course, he usually wore a cap. When I moved to the school in Largo do Leão, the second-year teacher, who had no idea how much I'd learned during my first year and had no reason to expect from my person any notable degree of knowledge (after all, why would she think any differently?), sent me to sit with the more backward children, who, given the way the room was arranged, were consigned to a kind of limbo, to the right of the teacher and facing the more advanced children, who were intended to serve as an example. A few days after classes had begun, the teacher, with the aim of finding out how familiar we were with the orthographic sciences, gave us a dictation. I had careful, round, very upright handwriting in those days, very good for a boy my age. Now it happened that I, Zezito (I'm not to blame for the diminutive, that's what my family called me, it would have been much worse if my name had been Manuel, then they would have called me Nelinho...), made just one mistake in the dictation, and even then it wasn't really a mistake, bearing in mind that all the letters of the word were there, but two had been transposed: instead of 'class' I had written 'calss'. Perhaps I was concentrating too hard. Anyway, now I come to think of it, that was where the story of my life began. (In our classroom, and probably in every classroom in the country, the double desks at which we sat were exactly the same as those which, fifty years later, in 1980, I found in the village school of Cidadelhe, in the region of Pinhel, when I was travelling around meeting people and places for my book *Journey to Portugal.* I confess that I couldn't conceal my emotion when I thought that, in times gone by, I might have sat at one of those desks. They were more decrepit and stained and scratched by use and lack of care, but it was as if they had been transported direct from Largo do Leão and 1929 to that village classroom.) But let's get back to the point of the story. The best student in the class occupied a desk right by the door and performed that most honourable of duties, class doorkeeper, for he was the one responsible for opening the door if anyone knocked. The teacher, surprised by the orthographic talent displayed by a boy who had just arrived from another school – and who was therefore assumed, by definition, to be a slacker – ordered me to go to the top of the class, where, of course, the dethroned monarch who had been sitting there until then had no alternative but to move. I can see the scene as if it were happening now, with me hastily gathering up my things, walking the length of the room before the perplexed (admiring? envious?) gaze of my classmates and, heart beating wildly, sitting down in my new place. When I won the PEN prize for my novel *Levantado do chão* [*Raised from the Ground*], I told this story to assure the audience that no moment of glory, present or future, could ever compare with that. Now, though, I can't help thinking about that other poor boy, coldly cast out by a teacher who must have known as much about teaching children as I did about subatomic particles, if such things were spoken of then. How would he explain to his parents – justifiably proud of their young son – that he had been knocked off his pedestal by a stranger who had just appeared over the horizon, like Tom Mix and Tony 'The Wonder Horse'? I can't remember whether I went on to become friends with my unfortunate class-mate, although he probably wanted nothing to do with me. Besides, if I remember rightly, shortly after that, I was transferred to another class, perhaps, who knows, to resolve the problem created by the teacher's lack of sensitivity. It isn't hard to imagine a furious father storming into the headmaster's office and protesting vehemently at the discrimination (did people use that word then?) of which his son had been the victim. Although, if truth be told, I have the impression that parents, in those primitive times, didn't worry overmuch about such details. It all came down to whether you got through the year or not, whether you passed or failed. Nothing else mattered.

When I moved from second year to third, Senhor Vairinho, the headmaster, summoned my father. He told him that I was a good, hard-working student and capable, therefore, of completing the third and fourth years in one year only. I would attend the normal third-year classes, while the more complex fourth-year subjects would be taught in private lessons given by Senhor Vairinho himself, who lived above the school. Given that this arrangement would cost him nothing, my father agreed, for Senhor Vairinho was doing it out of the goodness of his heart. I wasn't the sole beneficiary of this special treatment, three more of my classmates were in the same situation, two of whom came from quite well-off families. The only thing I remember about the third was that his mother was a widow. Of the other two, I recall that one was called Jorge and the other Maurício, but I can't even remember the name of the orphan, although I can still see his thin, rather bent figure. Jorge, I recollect, was already getting a beard. As for Maurício, he was a real devil in short trousers, quarrelsome, impetuous, always itching for a fight: once, in a fit of rage, he hurled himself on a classmate and stuck a pen in his chest. With a temperament like that, so quick to anger, what would have become of that boy in later life? We were friends, but not close. They never came to my house (well, living as we did, in rented rooms, it wouldn't even have occurred to me to invite them) and I was never invited to theirs. Any shared experiences, friendships and games were confined to the playground. By the way (was this perhaps another example of my presumed dyslexia?), I remember that, around this time, I confused the word '*retardador*' – 'delaying' – with '*redentor*' – 'redeeming' – and in the most bizarre manner imaginable. The slow-motion effect, which, in Portuguese, is '*o efeito de retardador*', had just begun to be used in films by then, or perhaps I'd only just noticed it. And during a game we were playing one day, I had to fall to the ground, but I decided to do it very slowly, saying: '*É o efeito redentor.*' The others took no notice, perhaps because that expression, which I had only just learned, wasn't familiar to them at all.

Out of school, I remember engaging in some terrific battles with children from the neighbouring houses, battles that involved much hurling of stones, but which, fortunately, never ended in blood and tears, although there was no shortage of sweat. As shields we had saucepan lids that we found among the rubbish. Now, I've never been particularly brave, but I remember once going on the attack beneath a hail of stones and how that one heroic gesture routed the two or three enemies opposing us. Even now, I have the sense that in advancing like that, bare-faced, I was disobeying one of the unspoken rules of engagement, that each army should stay where it was and take aim at the other side from that position, with no charges or counter-charges. More than seventy years later, in an image shrouded in the mists of memory, I can see myself with a saucepan lid in my left hand and a stone in my right (plus two more in my pockets), while missiles from both sides flew over my head.

What I remember most vividly about Senhor Vairinho's classes is the moment when, at the end of the lesson, with his four students lined up in front of his desk on the stage, he would write that day's marks in his beautiful hand in our black-bound exercise books, abbreviating the marks to B, A, G, E: bad, average, good, excellent. I still have that exercise book and it shows what a good student I was: there were very few 'bads', not many 'averages', lots of 'goods' and a fair number of 'excellents'. My father would sign at the bottom of the page each day, signing himself Sousa, because he never liked the Saramago he had been obliged to adopt by his son. It was a source of great pride to my family, both in the city and the village, that I passed the fourth-year exam with distinction. The oral exam took place in a ground-floor room (well, it was ground-floor in relation to the back of the building, which gave onto the playground, but first-floor in relation to the street) on a morning of brilliant sunshine, with a breeze wafting in through the windows open on either side, the trees in the playground looking green and leafy (I would never play in their shade again), and with my new suit, if my memory can be trusted, pinching me under the arms. I remember hesitating over one question from the jury (perhaps I didn't know the answer, perhaps my stutter had tied my tongue, as sometimes happened), and someone, a fairly young man whom I had never before seen in the school and who was standing just three steps from me, leaning against the frame of the nearest door – one of the doors that opened out onto the playground – whispered the response to me. Why was he there and not inside the room with everyone else? A mystery. That was in June of 1933, and in October, I would go to Liceu Gil Vicente, which was based then in the former monastery of São Vicente de Fora. For some time, I thought that the two went together, the name of the school and the name of the saint. I could hardly have been expected to know who Gil Vicente was.

I suppose (I can't be sure) that it was thanks to those 'lessons' gleaned from the Portuguese–French conversation guide and to my retentive memory that I managed to shine at my new school the very first time I was called to the blackboard, where I wrote the word *papier* and a few others with such ease that the teacher could not conceal his satisfaction, thinking, perhaps, that he had before him an expert in the language of Molière. When he told me to sit down again, such was my pleasure at having cut a good figure that, as I left the platform, I couldn't resist pulling a face to amuse my classmates. It was done purely out of nervousness, but the teacher must have interpreted it as an indication of future behaviour and he warned me at once that he was going to mark me down. This was a shame, because I hadn't done anything so very wrong. Later, however, he realised that he did not, in fact, have a professional agitator in his class and amended his earlier suspicions. As new recruits into the first year, we didn't know the teachers' names and so were disconcerted when the mathematics teacher, without introducing himself, merely informed us that he was the author of the book we would be studying from. Of course, no one dared to asked: 'But what's your *name*, sir?' It was a porter who came to our rescue. The teacher's name was Germano. I can't remember his surname.

During my first year, I was a good student in all subjects, with the exception of Choral Singing, which I only ever scraped through. My reputation reached such heights that, occasionally, older students would come into our classroom and ask which one was Saramago, I presume because they'd heard their teachers mention me. (This was the happy time when my father would always carry a piece of paper in his pocket to show his friends, a scrap of paper with my marks typewritten on it, beneath the heading 'My champ's marks'. In capitals.) My reputation reached such extravagant proportions that, at the beginning of the second year, when there were elections to the Academic Association, I was elected, if you please, to the post of treasurer. At the age of twelve. I remember being handed a pile of papers (subscriptions and balance sheets) which I barely understood and which, in fact, served no purpose whatsoever. My second year went badly. I don't know what was going on inside my head, maybe I'd begun to suspect that my feet were not intended for that road or perhaps I'd exhausted the store of energy I'd brought with me from primary school. Also, my father had started to work out the cost of it all, of a complete secondary school education, and to what end? My marks that year were generally low. In mathematics, for example, I didn't get a single pass in the first term or the second, and if I got quite a high mark in the third term, that leap – which would allow me to sit the exam – was not, I can assure you, due to some final, desperate flurry of activity on my part. Not at all. On the day when he announced the marks he intended to give us, the mathematics teacher had the very nice idea of asking the class as a whole if they thought I knew more about the science of numbers than my low marks would seem to indicate, and my classmates, in a display of solidarity and unanimity, replied: 'Yes, sir, he does.' Although the fact is, I didn't.

The entrance to the Liceu Gil Vicente was via a ramp that ran parallel with the narrow road that connects Largo de São Vicente to Campo de Santa Clara. The main door opened immediately onto a large walled area which was where we gathered at break time. I remember it as an enormous space (I don't know what it's like today, or if, indeed, it still exists) and have the idea that all the students, from first year to seventh, would have fitted in with room to spare. Once, as I mentioned earlier, I took such a tumble in the yard that I cut open my knee and bore the scar for many years. I was taken to the doctor's, and the male nurse (there was always a nurse on duty) applied a kind of clamp, known as a *gato*, to the wound. I described this *gato* earlier and I'll just give a few more details here. It was a small, narrow, rectangular piece of metal, which at first sight resembled an ordinary piece of tin, with the ends bent at right angles, and these would be pressed down on the edges of the wound and then gently squeezed until the edges met, thus helping the torn tissues to heal more quickly. I vividly remember the impression it made on me to see (and feel, although it wasn't that painful) the metal pressing into the skin. Afterwards, I had to walk around with a bandaged knee and a stiff leg until I went back to the doctor's for the *gato* to be removed. Another very vivid memory is of the pincers delicately extracting the piece of metal and the two marks it left behind, raw but not bleeding. I was ready for my next fall.

I remember with almost photographic clarity the school's long, broad corridors and the dark floor made of red tiles that appeared to have been waxed, although they may not have been, because it would have been a hard and thankless task to keep those floors clean when there were boots and shoes tramping along them all day, but if they weren't waxed, I can't explain how they were kept so shiny. There were never any marks on the wall, no litter, no cigarette ends, none of the commonplace abuses or youthful indifference you see now, as if time, since then, had judged these things to be vital elements in any really excellent education. Perhaps we learned discipline in the classes on Moral and Civic Instruction, although, to be honest, I can't remember a single one of the precepts we were given. Who was the teacher? I can't remember, I only know that he wasn't a priest and that religion wasn't taught at the Liceu Gil Vicente. Unfortunately, these classes, however secular and republican, did not prevent me, during those two years, but especially in my second year there, from becoming the biggest liar I've had the misfortune to meet. I would lie for no reason, I lied right, left and centre, I lied about anything and nothing. Compulsive behaviour they would call it today. My father, for example, had never been a man to get mixed up in politics – although, as a representative of the authorities, he naturally had to obey his masters' voice and carry out their orders, not that he minded – but once, when I was walking along with a classmate (a skinny fellow with buck teeth, who had the same thing for lunch every day – an omelette sandwich) on the upper floor of the cloister that led to the corridor where the classrooms were, I told him that my father had bought a copy of António Ferro's book *Salazar* (a collection of interviews with Portugal's then dictator) at the Book Fair. I can't remember my classmate's name. What I do remember is his silence and the look he gave me: his family probably belonged on the other side of the political divide. Rather more forgivable was my tendency to invent the plots of films I had never seen. Between Penha de França, where we were living, and school, on what is now Avenida General Roçadas leading into Rua da Graça, there were two cinemas, the Salão Oriente and the Royal Cine, and I and my other classmates who lived in that area would stand studying the posters that could be found outside all cinemas at the time and which were illustrated with stills from the various films. From those eight or ten images I would concoct a complete story, with beginning, middle and end, and was doubtless aided in this mystifying art by the knowledge I had acquired early on during the golden age of the Fleapit in the Mouraria. Slightly envious, my companions would listen attentively, asking the occasional question to clarify anything that didn't quite make sense, and I would heap lie upon lie, almost believing that I really had seen what I was merely inventing...

When I started going to the Liceu Gil Vicente, we were still living in Rua dos Heróis de Quionga. I'm sure this is so because I can remember, a few days after starting classes there, sitting on the floor reading my French book in a room that wasn't my parents' bedroom (by then, we had gone up a rung on the social ladder, and were renting a small apartment). We lived in Rua dos Heróis de Quionga along with the Baratas, who had come with us from Rua Fernão Lopes, bringing with them an elderly aunt of theirs (although where she came from I have no idea), who was called Emília, like the wife of Barata senior. Every now and then, about once or twice a month, the Baratas would receive a visit from a relative of theirs, a nephew or cousin called Júlio, who was blind and lived in some kind of institution. He wore a faded grey cotton uniform. He had a beardless face and what little hair was left on his head was cropped short, his eyes were almost white and he had the look of someone who masturbated every day (that's what I think now, not what I thought then), but what I disliked most about him was the smell he gave off, a rancid odour of cold, sad food and ill-washed clothes, a smell that would be associated for ever in my mind with blindness and which probably resurfaced later in my novel of that name. He would hug me very hard and I didn't like that either. Nevertheless, whenever I saw that he was about to write something, I would always go over and sit down next to him. He would place a sheet of thick paper, his own, between two metal trays and then, quickly, unhesitatingly, start pricking it with a kind of punch, as if he had perfect sight. I like to think that this 'writing' was a way of lighting stars in the unremitting dark of his blindness.

The present-bearing Three Wise Men didn't exist in those days (or is it just that I don't remember them?) nor did people make crèches with a cow and a donkey and everything. At least not in our house. You would leave a shoe by the fireplace, beside the oil stoves and, in the morning, you would go and see what Baby Jesus had left for you. Yes, it was Baby Jesus who came down the chimney then, he didn't just lie in the straw, belly button on view, waiting for the shepherds to bring him some milk and cheese, because he would need those to survive, not the gold-incense-and-myrrh of the Magi, who, as we know, only brought him things bitter to the tongue. In those days, Baby Jesus was a worker, who tried to be useful to society, a proletarian like the rest of us. Nevertheless, we children had our doubts; it was hard to believe that Baby Jesus would be prepared to soil his white clothes spending all night going up and down soot-begrimed chimneys. One Christmas Eve, perhaps because we had let slip a hint of this healthy scepticism, the grown-ups tried to convince us that the supernatural not only existed, it existed right there in our house. Two of them – it must have been two, possibly my father and António Barata – went out into the corridor and started pushing toy cars back and forth, from one end to the other, while the grown-ups who had stayed with us in the kitchen said: 'Can you hear? It's the angels.' Now I knew that corridor as well as if I had been born in it and had never noticed any angelic presence there when, for example, placing feet and hands on either wall, I would climb up until I could touch the ceiling with my head. I had never come across a single angel or seraph up there. Later on, when I was an adolescent, I tried to repeat that wall-climbing trick, but couldn't. My legs had grown longer, the joints in my ankles and knees less flexible. Ah, the weight of age...

Another memory (which I wrote about in *The Manual of Painting and Calligraphy*) involves the troubling case of Aunt Emília, who, as I said earlier, was an elderly lady, who wore her white hair in a bun at the back of her neck, a robust figure, very erect, with a naturally high colour made still higher by too much drink, and who always seemed to me exceptionally clean and neat. When it was the season, she used to sell roast chestnuts outside the bar a little further down the street, on the corner of Rua Morais Soares and Rua dos Heróis de Quionga, as well as other titbits – boiled sweets, honey-and-almond bars, loose almonds, and strings of pine-nuts that we called necklaces – that she set out on the tray with folding legs that she used. She would sometimes drink too much wine and get drunk. One day, the other women in the house found her lying on her back on the floor of her room, with her legs spread and her skirt up, singing some song or other while she masturbated. I tried to see what was going on, but the women formed a barrier to block my view. I must have been at most nine years old. It was one of the first chapters in my elementary sexual education.

A third and no less edifying affair was the skill with which people at home deceived the Water Company. They would make a tiny hole in an exposed part of the lead pipe then tie a rag around it, leaving one end hanging down into a pot. The pot would slowly fill up, drop by drop, and because that water didn't pass through the meter, it didn't appear on the bill. When the decanting process was over, that is, when the pot was full, they would run the blade of a knife over the tiny hole, and under this slight pressure, the lead itself would conceal the crime. I don't know how long this went on for, but eventually, the pipe, after multiple piercings, would refuse to remain an accomplice to the fraud and begin spurting water from every orifice, old and new. Then the 'man from the Water Company' had to be summoned urgently. He came, looked, cut into the damaged section of pipe and, not wishing to reveal that he knew all about a trick that could hardly have been new to him, peered inside the pipe and said: 'Yep, it's rotten, all right.' He would solder on a new piece of pipe and leave. He must have been a kind man because he clearly didn't want to get us into trouble by reporting us to the Water Company. As far as I recall, none of the three heads of household was ever present on those occasions, which was just as well, because it wouldn't have been easy to explain how we dared commit such illegal acts with two policemen on the premises, one of whom, more-over, worked in the Criminal Investigation Department. Another hypothesis that might merit serious considera-tion is that the Water Company employee had already had a word with my father or with one of the other two men and was in on the plot. It could be.

I have little else to say about our time in Rua Heróis de Quionga, just a few random memories of little importance: the cockroaches that scampered over me when I was sleeping on the floor; the way we used to eat soup, my mother and I, from the same plate, one on either side, taking it in turns to dip in our spoons; the morning it rained heavily and I refused to go to school, to my mother's fury and to my own even greater surprise that I would dare to miss classes when I wasn't ill and had no real reason for doing so; sitting at the windows that gave onto the long balcony at the back of the house, watching the raindrops trickling down the panes; looking through the imperfections in the glass at the distorted images these produced; the bread rolls bought from the bakery, still hot and delicious-smelling, and which we called '*sete e meios*' – 'seven-and-a-halfs', and the more expensive *vianinhas* made from finer flour and that I only rarely had the sweet satisfaction of eating... I've always loved bread.

Contrary to what I said earlier, the Barata family did not first enter my life when we moved from Rua dos Cavaleiros to Rua Fernão Lopes. Thanks to some documents I had assumed lost, but which providentially turned up when I was searching for something else entirely, my disoriented memory has finally been able to fit together various disparate pieces of the puzzle and replace what was uncertain and doubtful with what was right and true. Here then, for the record, is the exact and definitive list of our frequent changes of residence: we started out in a place known as Quinta do Perna-de-Pau, in the Picheleira district of Lisbon, then moved to Rua E (which later became Rua Luís Monteiro) in Alto do Pina, and from there to Rua Sabino de Sousa, followed by Rua Carrilho Videira (that's where the Baratas appear for the first time), Rua dos Cavaleiros (without the Baratas), Rua Fernão Lopes (with the Baratas again), Rua Heróis de Quionga (still with them), back to the same house in Rua Carrilho Videira (again with the Baratas), then to Rua Padre Sena Freitas (with only António Barata and Conceição), and finally to Rua Carlos Ribeiro (independent at last). Ten homes in just under ten years, and I don't think it was because we couldn't pay the rent. As you see, I was quite right when I said that we had lived in

Rua Carrilho Videira twice, but I made a serious miscalculation when, forgetting a few basic matters of sexual physiology and hormonal development, I added that I was eleven at the time of that encounter with Domitília. I got that completely wrong. In fact, I could only have been six at the time and she would have been about eight. If I had been eleven, and tall for my age too, she would have been thirteen, and in that case the whole affair would have been much more serious and the punishment for the crime rather more than a couple of slaps on the bottom. Anyway, now that I've sorted that out and the weight of error has been lifted from my conscience, I can continue.

In those days, when people couldn't afford to pay for a removal van, they would employ '*moços-de-fretes*' – 'porters' – whose only equipment was a couple of poles, some rope and a shoulder pad apiece to bear the weight. And, of course, a great deal of stamina. But they didn't transport the smaller things, which is why my mother, over the years (I'm not imagining this, I saw it with my own eyes), had to trudge miles back and forth between the different houses, carrying baskets and bundles on her head, or balanced on her hip if that was easier. Perhaps on one such occasion she would have recalled the day when, returning from the village fountain all confused and excited because my father had just asked her if they could be sweethearts, she forgot that she was carrying a water jug on her head and neglected to stoop down when going into the house. The jug struck the lintel and fell to the floor. Shards and water everywhere, my grandmother telling her off, then perhaps laughing when she found out the cause of the accident. You might say that my life started there too, with a broken water jug.

My mother arrived in Lisbon with us children in the spring of 1924. In December of that same year, Francisco died. He was four years old when bronchial pneumonia carried him off. He was buried on Christmas Eve. I don't really believe in so-called 'false memories', I think the difference between those and the memories we consider certain and solid is merely a question of confidence, the confidence that we place in the incorrigible vagueness we call certainty. Is the one memory I have of Francisco false? Perhaps, but I have spent the last eighty-three years believing it to be true. We are in a cellar in Rua E, in Alto do Pina, there is a chest of drawers underneath a horizontal opening in the wall, long and narrow, more of a slit than a window, level with the pavement outside (I can see people's legs through what must be a curtain), and the bottom two drawers are open, with the lower one pulled furthest out to form a step with the one above. It's the summer or perhaps the autumn of the year in which Francisco is going to die. At that moment (the photo is there for all to see), he is a happy, sturdy, perfect little boy, who, it would seem, cannot wait for his body to grow and for his arms to be long enough to reach something on top of the chest of drawers. That's all I can remember. Maybe my mother arrived to put a stop to Francisco's mountaineering ambitions, I don't know. I don't even know if she was at home, or if she had gone to scrub the steps of some neighbouring building. If she had to do that kind of work later on, out of necessity, when I was already grown up enough to understand what was happening, it's more than likely that she was doing it then, when the need was even greater. As Francisco's brother, I would have been unable to help the daring mountaineer had he fallen. I must have been sitting on the floor, dummy in my mouth, little more than eighteen months old, concerned, without even realising that I was, with recording what I was seeing in some part of my small brain so that, a whole lifetime later, I could describe it to you, dear reader. That, then, is my earliest memory. And it may well be false.

There is nothing false about what comes next however. The grief and the tears, could they be summoned up again, would bear testament to the fierce and violent truth. Francisco had already died and I must have been two or three years old. A short distance from the house (we were still living in Rua E at the time) there was a heap of rubble left over from some building work. Three or four older boys took me there by force (my small powers of resistance proved useless). They pushed me and threw me to the ground, removed my short trousers and my underpants, and, while the others held my arms and legs, one of them began to insert a piece of wire into my urethra. I screamed and struggled desperately, I kicked as hard as I could, but the cruel process continued, and the wire penetrated ever deeper. Perhaps the blood that started gushing from my small, suffering penis saved me from worse harm. The boys may have grown frightened or simply decided that they'd had their fun and fled. There was no one there to help me. Crying and with blood pouring down my legs, I left my clothes where they were on the rubble and staggered homewards. My mother had already come out to look for me (I can't remember what I was doing alone in the street), and when she saw me in that wretched state, she cried: 'Oh, my poor little boy! Who did this to you?', but all our tears and shouts were in vain, the guilty parties were far away by then, indeed, they may not even have lived in the area. Fortunately, the internal wounds healed up, because a piece of wire picked up from the ground seemed, in principle, a sure-fire recipe for tetanus. After

Francisco's death, it appeared that bad luck did not want to leave our door. I can imagine my parents' anxiety when, at the age of five, I developed a bad sore throat and they had to take me to the same hospital where Francisco had died. In the end, it turned out to be only an inflammation of the throat and sinusitis, nothing that couldn't be cured in a fortnight, which is precisely what happened. You may ask how it is that I know all these details when so much time has passed. It's a long story, but it can be summed up in a few words. When, many years ago now, I first had the idea of writing down my memories and experiences of the time when I was small, I thought immediately that I should speak of my brother Francisco's death (his life being so brief). Members of the family had always said that he died of what they called '*angina diftérica*', or 'croup' to use my mother's word, in the Instituto Bacteriológico Câmara Pestana. And yet, I cannot remember anyone mentioning the date of his death. I decided to investigate and wrote to the Instituto Câmara Pestana, and they very kindly responded, saying that they had no record of a child of four called

Francisco de Sousa. They sent me – I presume so as to make up for the disappointment – a copy of the record of my own admission on 4 April 1928 (I was discharged on the 11th of the same month), under the name of José Sousa, just like that, abbreviated twice. There's no trace of Saramago, and, as if that weren't enough, the preposition 'de' that should come between 'José' and 'Sousa' has also disappeared. Thanks to that piece of paper, though, I found out what my temperature was during those days of inflammation and sinusitis. I can clearly remember one visit from my parents. I had been placed in what was called the isolation ward, and we could only see each other through a glass window. I also remember sitting in bed and playing with a little clay burner and fanning the non-existent flame with a banana skin. I'd seen my mother doing much the same at home, and the truth is, that was about all I knew of life.

To return to my brother. As was only natural, the first thing I did, the very first, was to ask the registry office in Golegã, which dealt with our municipality, to send me the birth certificate of Francisco de Sousa, son of José de Sousa and Maria da Piedade from Azinhaga, because the date of his death should have appeared there. But it didn't. To judge from that official document, Francisco hadn't died. It was surprising enough to have the Instituto Bacteriólogico Câmara Pestana tell me, with due administrative seriousness, that he had never been admitted there, when I knew for certain that he had, but now it was the registry office in Golegã telling me, implicitly, that he was still alive. There was only one solution, to investigate the vast archives of the Lisbon cemeteries. Certain individuals offered to do this for me and for that I will be eternally grateful. Francisco died on 22 December at four in the afternoon and was buried in the Benfica cemetery on the 24th, at more or less the same time (what a sad Christmas that must have been for my parents). Francisco's story, however, does not end here. I doubt very much if my novel *All the Names* would be as it is if, in 1996, I hadn't become so well versed in the workings of registry offices...

His name was Francisco Carreira and he was a shoe-maker. His shop was a small, dark, windowless room, with a low door through which only children could enter without bending down, because it must have been, at most, about three or four feet high. He was always there, sitting on a stool behind a bench on which were laid out all the tools of his trade and which was covered with an ancient layer of dust and detritus: bent nails, shavings from soles, a blunt needle, a pair of broken pliers. He was a sick man, old before his time, with a deformed spine. All his strength was concentrated in his arms and shoulders, as strong as levers, and with them he could hammer on the sole of a shoe, wax the thread, pull the stitches tight and drive the tacks home with two short unerring blows. While I amused myself making holes in a piece of shoe leather with a punch or played with the water to which the soles of shoes, left to soak, lent an astringent touch of tannin, he would tell me tales of his youth: vague political plots, a pistol that had been shown to him as a sombre warning of what, word of honour, would happen to any traitor of the cause. Then he would ask me how school was going, what news I had of events in Lisbon, and I would waffle on as best I could to satisfy his curiosity. One day, he seemed preoccupied. He smoothed his thin hair with his bradawl and paused in his sewing, both of which were familiar signs, heralding a particularly important question. Shortly afterwards, Francisco Carreira leaned back his twisted body, pushed his glasses up onto his forehead and fired at point-blank range: 'Do you believe in the plurality of worlds?' He had read Fontenelle, and I had not, anything I did know having been gleaned from overhearing someone else discussing his work. I muttered something about the movement of the stars, mentioned Copernicus just in case, and that was that. But basically, yes, I did believe in the plurality of worlds, the main question being: was there anyone out there? He seemed pleased, or so it seemed to me, and I breathed a sigh of relief. Many years later, I wrote an article about him to which I gave the Lorca-inspired title, 'The Prodigious Shoemaker'. What other adjective could I have used? A shoemaker in my village, in the 1930s, talking about Fontenelle...

There was something I meant to say when, on an earlier page, I spoke about going to market with the pigs. My grandfather hadn't managed to sell many suckling pigs to his neighbours in Azinhaga that year, which is why he thought it best to take what remained of the litters to the market in Santarém. He asked if I would like to go along as my Uncle Manuel's assistant, and I didn't need to think twice, I said yes, I would. I greased my boots in preparation for the walk (this was not a journey to be undertaken barefoot) and went over to the porch to select a stick that best suited my height. We set off in mid-afternoon, my uncle at the rear, making sure none of the piglets went astray, and me at the front, with, at my heels, the sow who would keep them all together, the real mother of some of them and on maternal loan to the others for the occasion. Now and then my uncle would swap places with me, and then, like him, I had no alternative but to eat the dust kicked up by the livelier animals. It was almost dark by the time we reached Quinta da Cruz da Légua, where we had arranged to sleep. We put the pigs in a large shed and ate our food standing up in the light from a window, either because we preferred not to go into the house or, more likely, because the farm manager didn't invite us to. While we were eating, the servant came to say that we could sleep with the horses. He gave us two thick striped blankets and left. The stable door remained open, and that suited us well because we had to leave at dawn, before first light, in order to reach Santarém in time for the opening of the market. Our bed would be the two ends of the feeding trough that ran the length of the back wall. The horses snorted and stamped on the paved floor. I hoisted myself into the trough and lay down on the cool straw, as if in a cradle, wrapped in the blanket, breathing in the strong smell of the animals, who were restless all night or so it seemed to me in my fitful sleep. I felt tired, especially my legs and feet. The darkness was warm and thick, the horses shook their manes fiercely, and my uncle, his head almost touching my feet, was sleeping like a log. It was still dark when I awoke from the deep sleep to which I finally succumbed, and my uncle was calling to me: 'Come on, Zé, we've got to go.' I sat up in the trough, blinking and still sleepy, dazzled by an unexpected light. I jumped down and went out into the yard: before me, pouring a milky light over the night and the surrounding landscape, was a vast, round moon, making the white seem still whiter where the light struck it full on and the black shadows still deeper. I would never see a moon like that again. We fetched the pigs and set off very cautiously down into the valley, where the grass was very tall and there were thick shrubs and rocks, and the piglets, unused to being out so early, could easily stray and get lost. Once in the valley, it was much easier. We walked along a dusty path, the dust slaked by the cool of night, past vineyards in which the grapes were already ripe, and I leapt in among the vines and cut two large bunches that I slipped inside my shirt, looking around all the while in case a keeper should appear. I returned to the path and handed one of the bunches to my uncle. We walked on, eating the cold, sweet grapes, so hard they seemed almost crystallised. We started the climb up to Santarém when the sun was just coming up and spent all morning and part of the afternoon at the market. We did quite well, but still didn't manage to sell all the piglets. My uncle decided that we should return home via the low hills that rise up along that part of the Tejo, I can't remember why now, if, as seems unlikely, my uncle bothered to give me a reason. But it was thanks to that whim of his, that I encountered my first Roman road.

The rain is pouring down, the wind is shaking the leafless trees, and from times past comes an image, that of a tall, thin man, an old man, I realise, now that he draws nearer along the sodden track. He is carrying a crook over his shoulder and wears an ancient, muddy cape from which drip all the rains of heaven. Before him go the pigs, heads down, snouts to the ground. The man approaching, blurred amongst the teeming rain, is my grandfather. He looks weary. He bears on his back seventy years of a hard life full of privations and ignorance. And yet he is a wise man, taciturn, one who only opens his mouth to speak when necessary. Indeed, he speaks so little that we all fall silent to hear him when a kind of warning light illumines his face. He has a strange way of gazing into the distance, even if the distance is only the wall in front of him. His face, fixed but expressive, seems to have been carved out by an adze, and his small, sharp eyes shine sometimes as if something he had long been pondering had finally been understood. He is a man like many others on this earth, in this world, perhaps an Einstein crushed beneath a mountain of impossibilities, a philosopher, a great illiterate writer. Something he could never be. I remember those warm summer nights, when we slept under the big fig tree, I can hear him talking about the life he's led, about the Milky Way, or the Road to Santiago as we villagers still called it, that glowed above our heads, about the livestock he reared, about stories and legends from his remote childhood. We would fall asleep late, well wrapped up in our blankets against the dawn chill. But the image I can't shake off at this melancholy hour is of that old man advancing beneath the rain, stubborn, silent, like someone fulfilling a destiny nothing can change, except death. This old man, whom I can almost touch with my hand, doesn't know how he will die. He doesn't yet know that a few days before his final day, he will have a presentiment that the end has come and will go from tree to tree in his garden, embracing their trunks and saying goodbye to them, to their friendly shade, to the fruits he will never eat again. Because the great shadow will have arrived, until memory brings him back to life and finds him walking along that sodden path or lying beneath the dome of the sky and the eternally questioning stars. What word will he utter then?

There you were, grandma, sitting on the sill outside your house, open to the vast, starry night, to the sky of which you knew nothing and through which you would never travel, to the silence of the fields and the shadowy trees, and you said, with all the serenity of your ninety years and the fire of an adolescence never lost: 'The world is so beautiful, it makes me sad to think I have to die.' In those exact words. I was there.

Among the new-born piglets there would be the occasional weakling that would inevitably suffer with the night cold, especially in winter, which could prove fatal.

However, as far as I know, no such piglet ever died. Every night, my grandfather and grandmother would go to the sty to find the weakest of the piglets, wash their feet and legs and lay them down in their own bed. They would sleep there together, beneath the same blankets and the same sheets, with my grandmother on one side of the bed and my grandfather on the other, and between them, three or four piglets who must have thought they were in heaven.

The yard was divided into two parts that were different in shape and size. You could get to the first – the smaller one, which was more or less square – by the two stone steps outside the kitchen door or through a gate that opened directly onto the street and whose main purpose was in fact to let the pigs through, when, at the first light of dawn, my grandfather went out with them or when, almost at sunset, he brought them home again. We used it as well, of course, but for the animals it was the only way in and out. In that part of the yard, under a lean-to that always seemed to me to be on the point of collapse, were the pigsties, about four or five, where the sows lay, their teats exposed, suckling their young, and where they would sleep all night and as much of the day as the piglets would let them. All you had to do was open the doors of the pigsties for each sow to enter the appropriate one, taking her respective litter with her. I can't remember them ever once making a mistake, but it was not unknown for one or more of the piglets, blind with impatience, to go through the wrong door. They didn't stay there long. Incredible though it must seem to anyone who has never seen such things or heard tell of them, the sow knew each piglet from the way it sucked at the teat, and so she would use her snout to eject any interlopers. It would have made more of an impact had she bitten them, but I never saw that happen. The poor piglet had discovered, too late, that this was not his mother and he would squeal in distress for someone to help him. My grandfather or my grandmother would say to me: 'Zezito, go and sort him out, will you?' And I, an advanced student in matters of pig-breeding, would grab the intruder by one of its back legs, supporting it under the belly with my other hand, and take it back to its home sweet home, to the peace of hearing its real mother grunt with pleasure because the prodigal had returned. And how did I know which sty the stray belonged to? Nothing could be simpler. Each piglet had had a small amount of hair shaved off its body, one stripe for the first sty, two stripes for the second and so on. (Far more complex was the system of signs used by my grandmother to work out how much money she was spending at the grocer's, and I never knew her to be so much as a centavo out. In a notebook, she would draw circles with a cross inside them, circles with no cross, crosses outside the circles, dashes that she called 'sticks', and other symbols I cannot now recall. She would sometimes compare her own accounts with the list presented to her by the shopkeeper, Vieira, and often came out best. I will never forgive myself for not having asked her if I could have one of those notebooks for myself, for it would be documentary, even scientific proof that my grandmother Josefa had reinvented arithmetic, not that there's anything extraordinary or unusual about that in a family like mine, when one recalls that José Dinis solved the historic problem of squaring the circle when he was not yet ten years old.) Apart from the sties and the troughs where the pigs could enjoy their swill, sometimes enriched with a couple of handfuls of cornflour, there was also a hen-house, a rabbit hutch and a stable for the donkey. However hard you may try, there is never much to say about a hen-house, you simply hope that the chickens who live there get along well together and with the cockerel who covers them, that they produce eggs to sell, eggs that hatch to produce chicks, and eggs to eat at table on special occasions. My grandparents' hen-house was no exception, it had the same breeds any other hen-house would have, although doubtless fewer than most of them as regards the number of chickens and eggs produced. The rabbit hutch, on the other hand, does have a story. Uncle Carlos would visit it now and then, always at dead of night, in the brief intervals when he wasn't in the village lock-up in the square or hiding somewhere or other on suspicion of theft, especially of copper wire from telegraph poles, a highly prized commodity that he positively craved.

He wasn't a bad man, he just drank too much and had difficulty in distinguishing what was his from what was other people's. I don't think he preferred rabbit meat to chicken, it was simply that the rabbits were, shall we say, dumb, a couple of squeals and that was that, they didn't protest when grabbed by the ears and stuffed inside a sack, whereas the chickens were capable of kicking up a row that would wake the whole neighbourhood. My grandmother always got up when the still distant dawn was just a glimmer, and when she rose from her bed, she could consider herself very lucky indeed if Carlos Melrinho, as a filial souvenir of his latest nocturnal foray, had been charitable enough to leave her a rabbit or two. Unforgivable some will say, but it pays to know that not everything is as nice as pie even in the lives of the best families. Anyway, there are plenty of people out there who steal much more than copper wire and rabbits and still manage to pass themselves off as honest folk in the eyes of the world. In those times and in those places, things were what they appeared to be. Perhaps the one exception was the aforementioned stable for the donkey.

The name came from a time when it was, indeed, home to a female donkey I never knew. Despite the passing years, the name stayed, and just so that there should be no doubt about its beginnings, the hut still contained the old manger, as if the donkey's ghost were doomed to return each night to gorge on the memory of beans and straw. And apart from the bread oven that stood to one side of the kitchen door, the inventory of this part of the yard will be complete with the mention of the other pigsty, larger than those in which the sows and their litters would fit, although only just. This larger sty was home to the pig that had been chosen to be fattened up – although this didn't happen every year – an ungrateful beast whose bedding I, pitchfork in hand, would change at least once a week, removing the stinking straw, filthy with piss and shit, and replacing it with new straw that would take less than an hour to lose its natural freshness. One day, as I was engaged on this task, it began to rain, first a few fat, sparse drops, then hard and insistently. I thought it best to take shelter in the donkey's stable, but my grandfather's voice brought me up short: 'Finish what you've started. Rain only makes you wet, it doesn't break your bones.' He was right. I took up my pitchfork again and unhurriedly, patiently, like a good workman, completed the task, drenched, but happy.

A rough wattle-and-daub fence separated the two parts of the yard, with the inevitable gate to allow access to both. Immediately to the left stood the enormous stack of straw, with its typically pyramidal shape, a rectangular base narrowing towards the top, the clandestine fruit of my grandmother's dawn raids on the stubble in the wheatfields – carried out behind the keepers' backs – along with some of the other village women, all armed with a rake, a piece of cloth and some string. Next to it, so close that its branches touched the topmost part, was the big fig tree, or, quite simply, The Fig Tree, because although there was another one, it never grew very large, either because it wasn't in its nature to do so or out of respect for its veteran companion. There was also a venerable olive tree whose twisted trunk propped up the fence separating the two sections. Because of the brambles surrounding it and the hawthorn that stood menacing guard over it, that tree was the only one near my grandparents' house that I never climbed. There were a few more trees, although not that many, a couple of blackthorns that did the best they could, a rather miserly pomegranate, a few quince trees whose fruit you could smell ten paces away, a laurel and another olive tree or two. What little land remained was used for growing vegetables, especially kale, which sprouted all year round and therefore constituted the main ingredient in the local cuisine – boiled kale and haricot beans served with a little olive oil, and now and then, a plate of bread-crumbs made from cornbread fried in garlic with the main course served on top. The yard on this side was a narrow strip of land about one hundred and sixty to one hundred and seventy feet long, bordering an olive grove belonging to a man called Salvador and, on the other side, separating it from the street, grew a thick hedge made of reeds, brambles, the inevitable agaves and the occasional elder. From beneath that hedge I picked up, on two or three occasions, the dried skins that snakes had sloughed off when they no longer fitted them. The skins were good for some disease that afflicted pigs. Towards the end of that strip of land, it narrowed to a point, like the tail of a turtle. That was where my grandmother and I would go to do our business when we got caught short and didn't have time to go further into the olive grove. (My grandfather had to resolve the matter wherever he happened to be with the pigs.) And the reader should not be surprised by that euphemistic turn of phrase 'do our business'. It was the law of nature. Even Adam and Eve had to do their business in some corner of paradise.

The chest was decorated with blue oil paint, a somewhat drab colour like that of a rather grubby sky. It was in the outside room, next to the street door, on the right as you came in. It was big or, rather, enormous, it was the bean chest. My grandmother warned me not to open it because the dust from the beans caused terrible itching, covering the skin of anyone unwise enough to open the chest with *brotoeja*, which was the name we gave to the uncomfortable blisters that formed as a result. My grandfather, who had resolutely spartan ideas about complicated matters like character-building and fostering strength of mind, would chuckle at such warnings and concerns, and when he came home with the pigs at sunset, he would occasionally ask me if I had opened the chest yet.

I was not at the time, nor am I now, a great lover of that pruriginous legume, and so lifting the portentous lid of the chest just to peer in at some beans that were identical to other beans I could look at and handle without risk was not something that aroused my ten-year-old's curiosity, which was occupied with adventures of quite another calibre, such as exploring the banks of the Almonda and the Tejo or the labyrinthine tangle of undergrowth in Paul do Boquilobo. However, my grandfather's gentle irony, so often repeated, gradually wore away at my sensibility and provoked my young pride, so that one day, when I was alone in the house, I went over to the chest and, with a great effort, lifted the heavy lid as high as I could and then pushed it so that it fell with a thump against the whitewashed wall. There lay the beans. A little of the very fine dust veiling their beige skins had been stirred up with the sudden current of air and began to settle on my hands and forearms, where the promised skin eruption and itching would take only seconds to appear. However, as if the evolving state of my hands were not sufficient proof for my stubborn self, I plunged them in among the malignant beans, making the beans sift and rattle, and creating, this time, a veritable cloud of dust. This would be the moment to describe the ensuing itchy consequences if I did not have another tale to tell. As I moved round the chest towards one corner in order more easily to reach the upper edge of the lid and close it, I noticed that the lid itself was lined with newspaper. My grandparents' house was not a house of readers, for as I have said more than once, both were illiterate. If ever an uncle of mine came to stay, on leave from his military service for example, he would, if he could read at all, only be capable of deciphering the very largest and crudest of letters. The presence of those pages from *O Século* – which, quite rightly, announced on its masthead that it was the most widely read newspaper in the country, and I say 'quite rightly' because it was certainly the only newspaper to reach Azinhaga – the presence of those pages could only mean that my grandmother had asked Senhor João Vieira to save them for her once they'd been read and set aside in the shop where she was a regular customer. Had my grandparents been people with fine and delicate skin, I would admit the hypothesis that those sheets of paper were merely there to cover the very real cracks in the lid of the old chest and thus prevent the dangerous brown bean dust from treacherously attacking the defenceless tribe of the Melrinhos, the Caixinhas and the Saramagos. Another hypothesis, an artistic one this time, is that those letters, words and images were as attractive to my grandmother's eyes as, years later, Chinese or Arabic characters, for example, were to her grandson's. The mystery remains unresolved.

I was ten, but I could already read fluently and understand perfectly everything I read, and considering my tender age, I didn't make too many spelling mistakes either, not that this, at the time, was considered something deserving of a medal. You will understand, then, that despite the almost unbearable itching that cried out for the cool balsam of a bowl of cold water or a little vinegar, I seized the opportunity to plunge into the varied bit of reading that chance had placed in my path. It was the summer of 1933, and I was ten years old, and of all the news items published in *O Século* on a particular day of the previous year, I can remember only one: the photograph, with explanatory caption, that showed the Austrian Chancellor Dollfuss watching a parade of soldiers in Austria. This was the summer of 1933, and Hitler had taken power in Germany only six months before, but I have no recollection of having read about this in the *Diário de Notícias*, the newspaper my father used to bring back to our Lisbon home. I'm on holiday, in the house of my maternal grandparents, and while I absentmindedly scratch my arms, I feel surprised that a Chancellor (whatever a chancellor was) could be so short. Neither I nor Dollfuss know that the following year he will be assassinated by the Austrian Nazis.

Around this time (perhaps still in 1933 or possibly 1934, if I'm not getting my dates mixed up) as I was walking down Rua da Graça, on my accustomed route between Penha de França, where I was living, and São Vicente, where I went to school, I saw, hanging on the door of a tobacconist's shop, right opposite the old Royal Cine, a newspaper whose front page bore a perfect drawing of a hand reaching out to grab something. Underneath were the words: 'An iron hand in a velvet glove'. The newspaper in question was the satirical weekly *Sempre Fixe*, the artist Francisco Valença, and the hand was supposed to be Salazar's.

Don't ask me why, but those two images have stayed with me all my life – that of Dollfuss smiling as he watched the troops march past, when he had possibly, who knows, already been condemned to death by Hitler, and Salazar's iron hand concealed beneath a soft, velvet glove of hypocrisy. We often forget what we would like to remember, and yet certain images, words, flashes, illuminations repeatedly, obsessively return to us from the past at the slightest stimulus, and there's no explanation for that; we don't summon them up, they are simply there. And it is those memories that tell me that although, at the time, I was basing myself more on intuition than, of course, on any real knowledge of the facts, Hitler, Mussolini and Salazar were, in my view, all chips off the same block, first cousins, each with the same iron hand, the only difference being the thickness of the velvet and how tightly the hand could squeeze.

When the Spanish Civil War broke out, I had already moved from secondary school at the Liceu Gil Vicente to technical college at the Escola Industrial de Afonso Domingues, in Xabregas, and I was doing my best to learn, as well as Portuguese, mathematics, physics, chemistry, mechanical design, mechanics and history, a little French and literature (it amazes me to think that in those days they taught French and literature at a technical school) and, finally, which was the real reason I was there, to penetrate, little by little, into the mysteries of the profession of general mechanic. I read in the press that those on one side in the Spanish Civil War were known as reds and those on the other as nationalists, and since the newspapers published regular reports of the various battles, occasionally illustrated with maps, I decided, as I mentioned earlier, to create my own map, on which, depending on the result of each battle, I would stick different coloured flags, red and yellow, I believe, and thanks to which I imagined I was accompanying, to use the age-old expression, the development of operations. Then one day, quite early on, I realised that I was being mocked by the retired soldiers whose job it was to censor the press, respectfully making theirs the iron hand and the velvet glove. According to them, only Franco's victories counted. The map was thrown in the bin and the flags lost. And this was probably one reason why, when I was sent with my classmates to the Liceu de Camões, where the green and brown uniforms of the Mocidade Portuguesa – Portuguese Youth Movement – were being given out, I managed never to get beyond the end of the queue that stretched out into the street, and I was still there when a graduate (as the older boys were known) came to tell us that they had run out of uniforms. In the weeks that followed, there were more distributions of berets, shirts and shorts, but I, along with a few others, always went to parades in civvies, and showed myself to have two left feet when marching and to be as clumsy with a gun as I was inept at target shooting. That was not my destiny.

One of my schoolfriends was a plump, sad-looking boy with large round glasses, who always seemed to have a whiff of medicine about him. He often missed classes, but these absences were put down to ill health. We never knew if he would be there in the morning or if he would stay for the whole day. Despite this, he was intelligent and hard-working, and was one of the students who always got the highest marks. He was excused gym and could never take part in our rather rough games, and I never saw him in the playground at break time. He was brought to school by car and the same car came to pick him up. Since there was no refectory, the boys ate wherever they happened to be, in the corridors, in the playground, or in the gallery of the cloister on the floor occupied by the school. He, however, had a special dispensation from the headmaster, and his lunch was brought to him, still hot, by a maid and was served to him – complete with tablecloth and napkin – in a room on the ground floor, in peace, far from the noise and bustle. I felt rather sorry for him. And perhaps he noticed this because one day he asked if I would like to join him, not for lunch, of course, but to keep him company. I said that I would. We arranged that I would go and sit with him once I had eaten – upstairs – my usual bread roll filled with chouriço sausage, cheese or omelette, and then, once he, too, had finished his lunch, we would go up to the classroom together. With his round, sad face, he would sit chewing slowly, listlessly, deaf to the maid's pleas: 'Just a little bit more, *menino*, just a little bit more...' I immediately grasped the situation and, to cheer him up, started clowning around, pretending to trip over my own feet and so on, and my very elementary comic skills brought results. I made him laugh and then he would eat almost without realising, and the maid was delighted. He must have spoken about me to his parents because one day, he invited me to his house, which turned out to be a real mansion (well, to me it looked like a palace) in Calçada da Cruz da Pedra, above a terraced garden with views over the Tejo. I was welcomed by him and his youngest sister, although his mother only stayed with us for a few minutes and then left. It was tea time. We ate in a small room furnished in a style that reminded me of the Formigal household, albeit less solemn and with no damask. They tried to alarm me by placing under my cup and under the tablecloth a kind of balloon that could be inflated by my friend on the other side of the table squeezing a small rubber bulb. I saw the cup and saucer start to jig about, but I wasn't afraid. It was merely an effect for which I had to find the cause. I lifted the table cloth and we all burst out laughing. Then we went out into the garden to play *burro* (the name given to a game played on a sloping board marked out with numbered squares into which you had to throw a counter, the winner being the player with the largest number of points) and I lost. When I began studying at technical college, I went to his house for the last time. I showed him my student card with a display of pride I knew to be false (at the Liceu we didn't have such cards), but he merely gave it a bored, cursory glance. I never saw him again. The mansion was on my way to college, but I never made a point of going a few yards out of my way in order to knock on his door. I think I must have sensed that I had ceased to be useful to him.

One day, during a mechanics class, I broke a pointer. The teacher had not yet arrived and we were making the most of the opportunity to have a good time, some were telling jokes, others were throwing paper planes or balls of paper, still others were playing at 'palms' (a magnificent exercise for honing the reflexes, because the player holding his open palms out for the other player to strike has to move very fast to avoid the next blow), and I, intending to exemplify the use of the lance – why I don't know, perhaps because of some film I'd seen – grabbed the pointer and raced towards the blackboard, to which I'd given the role of the enemy to be unhorsed. I misjudged the distance and hit the board so hard that the pointer broke into three pieces in my hand. The incident was greeted with applause by some, but others fell silent and looked at me with that expression on their faces which means the same in every language in the world: 'You're for it now,' while I, as if I believed a miracle were possible, tried to fit the broken pieces of wood together again. When the miracle didn't happen, I was just depositing the remains on the teacher's dais when the teacher came in. 'What happened?' he asked. I came up with a hasty explanation ('The pointer was on the floor and I inadvertently stepped on it, sir') which he pretended to believe. 'Well, you'll have to buy another one,' he said. So it was and had to be. It didn't occur to anyone at home to go to a shop selling school equipment and ask how much a new one would cost. It was assumed that it would be far too expensive and that the best solution would be to go to a sawmill and buy a piece of wood of about the same size that I could then work on to produce something as similar as possible to the real pointer. And that's what happened. For good or ill, neither my father nor my mother got involved. Over a period of perhaps two weeks, including Saturday afternoons and Sundays, I slaved away with my knife like a condemned man, planing and sanding and filing and waxing the wretched piece of wood. My experience of working with tools at Azinhaga paid off. The final result was not what you might call perfection, but worthy enough to take the place of the broken original, and it won the necessary administrative approval and an understanding smile from my teacher. Bear in mind that my speciality was mechanics not carpentry.

José Dinis died young. Once the golden years of childhood were over, we had each gone our separate ways, then, some time later, when I was in Azinhaga, I asked Aunt Maria Elvira: 'What's José Dinis up to these days?' And she said quite simply: 'José Dinis died.' That's the way we were, we might be hurting inside, but we put up a hard front. Things are as they are, you're born, you live and you die, and there's no point making a fuss about it, José Dinis came and went, tears were shed at the time, but the fact is that people can't spend their entire lives grieving for the dead. I would like to think that no one now would remember José Dinis if these pages had not been written. I'm the only one who can remember how we used to balance rather precariously on the steps of the harvester and cross the field from end to end, watching as the machine cut down the ears of wheat and how we would get covered in dust in the process. I'm the only one who can still remember the superb watermelon with its dark green skin that we ate on the banks of the Tejo, because the melon patch was in the river itself, on one of those tongues of sandy soil, sometimes quite extensive, that were left exposed each summer when the volume of water diminished. I'm the only one who can remember the creak of the knife as it opened, the bright red slices and the black seeds, the 'castle' (in other places they call it the 'heart') that was left in the middle of the melon as we sliced away at the flesh (the knife wasn't long enough to reach the very centre of the fruit), and the way the juice trickled down your throat onto your chest. And I'm the only one who can remember the time I betrayed José Dinis. We were walking along with Aunt Maria Elvira, searching for corn, each with our own row to follow and a bag slung round our neck, breaking off the ears of corn that the pickers had inadvertently left on the stalks, and suddenly I spotted a huge ear of corn in José Dinis' row, but I said nothing, waiting to see if he would walk past without noticing it. When he, the victim of his small stature, did precisely that, I went and picked the cob. The fury of the poor plundered boy was a sight to see, but Aunt Maria Elvira and the other adults present said I was quite right, if he had seen it, I wouldn't have picked it. They were wrong. If I had been generous, I would have given him the corncob or said simply: 'Look, José Dinis, right there in front of you.' I could blame this on the constant state of rivalry we lived in, but I suspect that on the Final Day of Judgement, when my good and bad actions are placed in the balance, it will be the weight of that ear of corn that sends me down to hell...

A short distance from my grandparents' yard was a ruined farm building, what remained of some old pig pens. We used to call them Veiga's pig pens, and I would walk through them whenever I wanted to take a short-cut through the olive groves. One day, when I was about sixteen, I came across a woman in there, standing up among the weeds, pulling down her skirt, and a man buttoning up his trousers. I turned away and went and sat on a wall by the road, near an olive tree at the foot of which, a few days before, I had seen a large green lizard. After a few minutes, I saw the woman hurrying away through the olive grove opposite, almost running. The man emerged from the ruins, came over to me (he must have been a tractor driver brought in from outside to do a particular job) and sat down beside me. 'Nice woman,' he said. I didn't respond. The woman kept appearing and disappearing among the trunks of the olive trees, moving further off all the time. 'She said you know her and would tell her husband.' I still did not respond. The man lit a cigarette, blew the smoke out twice, then he let himself slide off the wall and said goodbye. 'Goodbye,' I said. The woman had finally disappeared from view. I never saw the green lizard again.

This is Francisco, the brother whose image I didn't dare to steal. He lived for such a short time, but who knows what he might have become. Sometimes I think that, by living, I have tried to give him life.

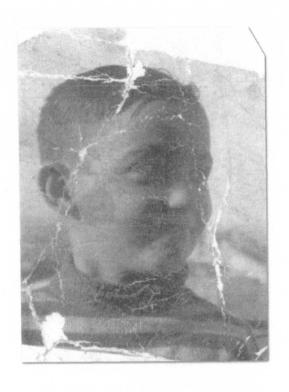

I am six years old and standing on the balcony at the back of the house in Rua Fernão Lopes. If my memory serves me right, beside me were António Barata and his wife; however, an implacable pair of scissors has separated me from them. My mother was always very clear where relationships were concerned: the end of a friendship meant the end of any photos too.

This dates from my primary school days. It is, I think, the second photograph taken of me, if I don't count the one that disappeared and in which I was pictured with my mother outside the grocer's shop, with her dressed in heavy mourning following the death of my brother Francisco and with me looking very sad.

They've put a tie on me in this one, and pinned the badge of Benfica football club to my lapel. My father made me a member of the club and used to take me to watch them play at the old Amoreiras stadium. This was more for his benefit than for mine. It was fun, but I was never that much of a fan.

There's a triumphal air about me here; I'm wearing a confident half-smile. I assume this was taken after the fourth-year exams, when I was already looking forward to the responsibilities that awaited me at secondary school.

The triumphal air didn't last.

I should perhaps have placed this photo earlier. I look rather fragile and delicate, in complete contrast to the positive and slightly smug expression of the previous picture. One thing, though, that doesn't quite fit with my theory that this is an earlier photo is the loosely knotted tie, a fashion that came in later.

Here I am, a fully-fledged adolescent. The Benfica badge has vanished, and I seem to recall that, by then, I had stopped going to matches. I've gone back to wearing my tie tightly knotted, a style that has accompanied me all my life, right up until the present day.

By now, I had a girlfriend. You can tell by the look

on my face.

In Azinhaga. Legs straddled, I gaze at the camera with a determined air. I didn't know what to do with my hands, so I stuck them in my pockets. Trouser pockets are the refuge of the shy.

Here they are, Josefa and Jerónimo. I find that hand on my grandmother's shoulder very touching. They didn't much go in for public displays of affection, but I know they loved each other and still did then.

My grandmother has a child in her arms, but I don't know

who it is. He looks to me like Uncle Manuel's son.

I'm not sure what to make of this gentleman. His face is that of my grandfather Jerónimo, but the suit isn't him at all. It was lent to him for the occasion by the husband of my Aunt Maria da Luz, who, at the time, lived in Oporto, where the photo was taken.

My mother was a beauty. It's not me who says so,

but the photo.

They made a handsome couple. My mother was pregnant with my brother Francisco at the time. I came along later, but there's no photo.

My father, when he'd already been promoted to sergeant.

He was what people used to call 'a fine figure of a man'.

So *beautiful!*

The years passed, and this is possibly the last photo of my father. Despite his various shenanigans, he was not a bad person. One day, when I was already a grown man, he said to me: 'Now you, you've always been a good son.' At that moment, I forgave him everything. We had never been so close before.

Translator's Acknowledgements

The translator would like to thank José Saramago, Tânia Ganho and Ben Sherriff for all their help and advice.